PSYCHOLOGY**TOOL**

Psychology tools
for overcoming panic

Matthew Whalley

Published by Psychology Tools

© 2017 Matthew Whalley

http://psychologytools.com

First edition 2017

ISBN 978-0-9932968-4-0

Cover artwork and design by Joseph Whittle

Disclaimer

This book is for information purposes only. Every effort has been made to ensure that the information it contains is accurate, but no guarantee can be given that it is free from error or omission. The information contained in this book is not a substitute for proper diagnosis, treatment, or provision of advice by a qualified health professional.

About

The author

Dr Matthew Whalley is a clinical psychologist working in the United Kingdom. He has held posts in primary, secondary, and community mental health teams, as well as in a health psychology service. He currently works in a specialist psychological trauma service in the NHS and has a particular interest in the treatment of anxiety. He has a background in psychological research – completing a PhD in psychology at University College London where he also completed postdoctoral research investigating memory in post-traumatic stress disorder (PTSD). He has published research in pain, PTSD, depression, and hypnosis. He is passionate about using the internet to make high-quality mental health information available to therapists and clients. To this end he has developed a number of web sites including Psychology Tools.

Psychology Tools

Psychology Tools (http://psychologytools.com) is a website targeted at psychological therapists around the world. Its mission is to make evidence-based tools and resources available to therapists and their clients. Volunteers have translated Psychology Tools materials into over 45 languages.

Table of contents

Introduction

Panic is a very common problem. It is estimated that nearly one in every four people will experience a panic attack at some point in their life, and between 3-4% of people will experience recurrent panic attacks (panic disorder).

The good news is that panic is very treatable. Research has shown that the most effective psychological treatment for panic is cognitive behavioral therapy (CBT). CBT is an evidence-based treatment for a variety of conditions including anxiety, depression, and trauma. It has been proven to be helpful for panic when delivered by a therapist face-to-face, or as self-help from a book or over the internet. This book introduces CBT for panic disorder and will give you a toolkit for overcoming your panic.

The book is split into five sections. Part 1 explores what panic attacks and panic disorder are. Part 2 introduces you to the CBT way of thinking about panic. Part 3 guides you through the exercises you need to do in order to overcome your panic disorder. Part 4 helps you think about what comes after panic disorder, and about how you can hold on to the improvements you have made. Part 5 is a collection of resources you can use to overcome your panic.

Part 1

What is panic disorder?

The experience of panic

Ted's story

Ted experienced his first panic attack during a stressful time in his life. His mother was in hospital and he had been rushing to complete some work so that he could leave on time to visit her. He was delayed on the way to the hospital and worried that he might miss visiting hours. As he walked down a corridor in the hospital Ted suddenly began to feel lightheaded and worried that he couldn't breathe properly. He felt a wave of fear come over him, noticed himself getting hot and sweaty, and felt an overwhelming urge to escape. He left the hospital quickly and smoked a cigarette in the car park to calm himself down. The sensations had only lasted a few minutes but to Ted it felt like forever.

Ted experienced more panic attacks over the next week. Each time they would come completely out of the blue and he would experience overwhelming sensations of dread and fear. He could feel his heart race and his throat getting tight. He worried that he wouldn't be able to get enough air and would pass out. He only felt better when he got out in the open and away from people. Ted stayed away from windowless buildings, crowds, and from anywhere busy. He started to avoid going to places where he had panicked before, and even took to doing his shopping at night when it was less busy.

Vanessa's story

Vanessa's life was even busier than normal while her husband was out of town, leaving her to care for their two small children. As she was driving them to school one morning Vanessa noticed her heart pounding – she could feel it beating in her chest. She began to sweat, and felt lightheaded. She wondered whether she was having a heart attack like her uncle had, and she had an image in her mind of her children attending her funeral. She pulled the car over to the side of the road and sat breathing, terrified, until the symptoms gradually passed.

Vanessa arranged an appointment with her doctor that afternoon. He examined her and conducted tests, but eventually told her it was probably just anxiety and that she shouldn't worry. Her worry didn't disappear though. She cut back on any activities she felt were dangerous or unnecessary. She stopped driving and insisted that her husband take the children to school for fear that she might have an accident. She also stopped exercising for fear it could trigger a heart attack.

People with panic disorder have sudden and repeated attacks of fear. These panic attacks are accompanied by strong physical reactions, such as a racing heartbeat, sweating, shaking, and thoughts that something terrible is happening or will happen. Panic attacks can happen at any time, and people who have experienced a panic attack often dread the possibility of having another one. It is common for sufferers of panic attacks to take steps to try to prevent further attacks from happening.

What is a panic attack?

Panic attacks are a sudden surge of intense fear or discomfort that reaches a peak within seconds to minutes. Panic attacks involve feeling at least four of the following symptoms:

- Palpitations, pounding heart, or accelerated heart rate

- Sweating

- Trembling or shaking

- Sensations of shortness of breath or smothering

- Feeling of choking

- Chest pain or discomfort

- Nausea or abdominal distress (e.g. diarrhea)

- Feeling dizzy, unsteady, lightheaded, or faint

- Chills or heat sensations

- Paresthesias (numbness or tingling sensations)

- Derealization (feelings of unreality) or depersonalization (feeling of being detached from oneself)

- Fear of losing control or going crazy

- Fear of dying

How many of these have you experienced? These symptoms can be terrifying, especially if they come out of the blue. Many people with panic are surprised that symptoms of anxiety can be so strong. Some end up having health check-ups to rule out physical causes for their symptoms.

Some people might just have a one-off panic attack and never experience any more. However, having experienced one panic attack makes you more likely to have another at some point in the future.

How is panic disorder different from a panic attack?

Panic attacks are single episodes of intense fear. They are very common, especially in people who suffer from anxiety disorders. People get the diagnosis of *panic disorder* when they have:

- Had more than one sudden and unexpected panic attack

- Worry a lot about the prospect of having another one

- Take precautions to avoid having another panic attack, such as avoiding places where previous panic attacks have happened

Panic attacks are unpleasant in the short term but tend to pass quite quickly. Panic disorder affects people's live more significantly. People with panic disorder find that even when they are not panicking they tend to worry about future panic attacks and their implications.

Some people find that they continue to experience unexpected panic attacks whereas others start to notice patterns in where and when they experience panic.

What causes panic?

Panic is rarely caused by one single thing. A better way to think about panic is shown in the diagram below. There may be things about us that make us *vulnerable* to developing panic at some point in our lives. *Stresses and triggers* explain why panic visits us now rather than at another time in our lives. Once we have panic there are common things that people typically do to cope with the unpleasant feelings it brings. Unfortunately some of the most common *coping strategies*, while improving how you feel in the short-term, have *unintended consequences* which may result in more panic attacks.

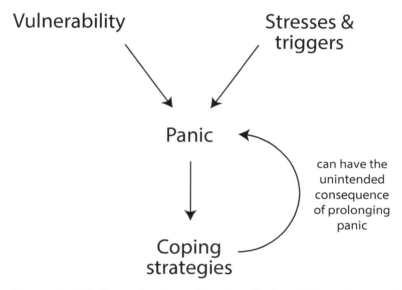

Figure: Panic is the result of a combination of vulnerability and stress. Our coping strategies intended to prevent panic can sometimes lead to having more panic attacks.

Vulnerability to panic

Both biological and psychological factors can make some people more vulnerable to panic. It is important to know right away that there is nothing terribly 'wrong' with people who experience panic. Panic is not thought to be the result of any neurochemical imbalance, nor any major biological dysfunction. Panic does not 'run in families' like hair color or height, although there is some evidence that having a family member with panic makes you somewhat more likely to experience panic yourself.

Everybody's nervous system is different, and people who are vulnerable to panic are thought to have nervous systems which are more sensitive than others. Psychologists call this 'body vigilance' and it simply means that people who panic are often more able than others to be aware of what is going on in their bodies. Having this ability is probably helpful in many ways – it might stop us getting too hot, cold, hungry, or thirsty. In people who panic it may just be turned up too high.

Psychological factors play a big role in panic. The way we think directly affects the way we feel and so our beliefs are critically important. People with certain beliefs about physical sensations tend to be particularly afraid of them. For example, Ted worried that tightness in his throat meant he would suffocate, and Vanessa worried that her racing heat meant she would have a heart attack. Beliefs that particular body sensations are harmful, or will lead to some kind of catastrophe, tend to be the most anxiety-provoking. We are not born with our beliefs, but develop them through our personal experiences. We can learn them from what other people say or do, or from things we observe and experience. Personal experiences of illness or loss, either our own or people close to us, often lead to the development of particularly strong beliefs.

Stresses and triggers leading to panic

Stress also plays a key role in panic. People often experience their first panic attack at a particularly stressful moment in their life. Negative events such as relationship problems, work difficulties, or money worries are obviously stressful. Positive events such as buying a house, starting a new job, or going on a date can be stressful too. Everyone responds differently to stress, and what is stressful for one person may not be stressful for another. Stress is really anything which pushes us outside our own personal comfort zone. The diagram below shows why we are more likely to experience panic if we are already under a lot of stress. If we start off calm then it takes quite a lot to get us into the 'panic zone', but if we are already under pressure then it might only take a small trigger.

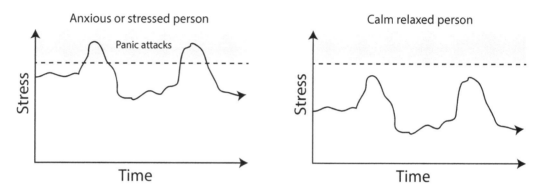

Figure: Stress is an unavoidable part of life. Events are more likely to lead to panic attacks if we are generally stressed, anxious, or under a lot of pressure.

Our best efforts to cope can cause panic

Nobody likes feeling upset, afraid, or anxious. Human beings have instinctive and automatic ways of coping with some of our more powerful feelings. We generally try our best to cope with how we are feeling and most of us have our favourite or habitual ways of soothing ourselves. Unfortunately, some of the ways we choose to deal with panic can be counterproductive – they can actually result in more panic. Unhelpful coping strategies include avoidance, 'safety behaviors', and drugs or alcohol. We will examine the effects of these in more detail in the next section.

Part 2

The CBT way of thinking about panic

Introduction to CBT

Cognitive Behavioral Therapy (CBT) is both a form of psychological therapy, and a very helpful way of thinking about human experiences. It gives us a set of tools to break down people's problems in a way which leads us towards helpful solutions. The basic idea of CBT is simple but powerful: CBT says that what we think and do affects the way we feel.

Figure: The basic message of CBT: What we think and do affects the way we feel

The CBT model

CBT is interested in our thoughts, actions, and feelings. Any situation or problem can be broken down into four key parts:

- Thoughts – What was going through your mind?

- Emotions – How did you feel emotionally?

- Body sensations – What did you feel in your body?

- Behavior – What did you do? How did you react?

Importantly, each of these parts can affect any of the others.

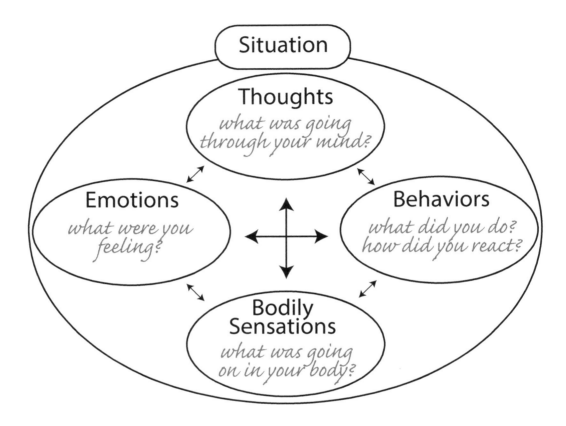

Figure: Any situation can be broken down into what was happening (situation), what we thought, what we felt (emotionally), what we felt in our bodies (physical sensations), and how we reacted. Each of these things can affect any of the others.

Let's think of some examples. Suppose Ted hears a noise in the middle of the night. He thinks to himself *"It's a burglar – I'm being robbed!"*. He is immediately on alert and feeling frightened, and he feels his heart pound, his muscles tense, and his breathing get quicker. Ted starts looking for something to defend himself with.

Let's imagine that Ted reacts differently. Suppose a noise startles him awake in the middle of the night but this time he thinks to himself *"It's just the neighbourhood cats knocking things over in the alley"*. He does not feel any fear, and feels relaxed in his body. He turns over and goes back to sleep.

Notice how the same event, a noise in the middle of the night, can be interpreted in different ways. Different feelings and consequences flow from these different interpretations. This basic principle of CBT, that what we think affects the way we feel, has important consequences for how we react to any situation. This is especially true for situations in which we panic.

Throughout the rest of this book we will think about panic using this model. In the next sections we will look at the roles of thoughts, emotions, body sensations, and behaviors in panic.

Emotions in panic

Emotions are a fundamental part of being human. Imagine not having any emotions: how would you know what is important and what isn't?

What are emotions for?

One purpose of emotion is to motivate us to take action. For example, feeling happy makes us want to do more of whatever we are doing. Feeling guilty makes us want to put right mistakes we have made. Feeling frightened typically makes us want to get away from whatever is making us afraid.

Simple emotions such as happiness, sadness, or fear are very old in biological terms. The parts of the brain that deal with these emotions are more basic than the parts that deal with logic and reason. This matters because it explains how 'convincing' our emotions can be, and how overwhelming it can be to feel strong feelings. However, just because feelings are strong it does not mean that they always have our best interests at heart: what feels 'easy' and 'the right thing to do' are often quite different. Furthermore, many psychological problems get worse when we take action based on unhelpful feelings.

The purpose of fear

The key emotion in panic disorder is fear. When we have a panic attack we are afraid that something terrible is happening or will happen. Anxiety is an umbrella term for feelings of fear, nervousness, apprehensiveness, or worry. Anxiety is a completely natural response to things that we find threatening. Threats can be physical, such as accidents or violence; social such as rejection or humiliation; or mental such as the possibility of losing control of your mind. Although threats can be real, anxiety by itself is not dangerous. Everybody gets anxious at times and some anxiety actually helps us to function at our best. Anxiety only interferes with our lives when:

- It happens too often

- It goes on for a long time

- It stops us from doing things that we want to do

Why is having some anxiety a good thing?

People suffering from anxiety often want to get rid of it completely. Although this might sound attractive it would not be a sensible plan. Imagine never being anxious or nervous: how would you know how to take care of yourself? For example, how would you know not to run across a busy road? Or to mind your footing when walking along the edge of a cliff? Or to be cautious when approaching a wild animal? Feelings of anxiety can guide us to take care of ourselves. Researchers have found that just the right amount of anxiety actually helps us to perform at our best. This is true of athletes competing, musicians performing, students taking an exam, or you and me in our daily lives. The diagram below shows why having some anxiety is a good thing.

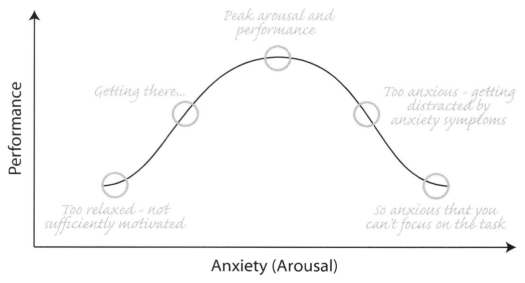

Figure: Increased anxiety helps us to perform better, but only up to a certain point

Body sensations in panic

The number one job of all living things is to *survive*. The bodies and minds of human beings and other animals have evolved finely tuned systems to protect them from threats. These systems have helped them to survive over thousands of generations. Let's have a think about how it works. Imagine a caveman is out hunting for his dinner when he comes across a tiger.

Q: What are the caveman's best options for survival?

A: Fight, run away, or stay very still

Human beings and many other animals are evolved to deal with precisely these kinds of dangerous situations. There are typically only a limited range of helpful behaviours in situations where you face a physical threat. These include:

Fight	Run away ('take flight')	Freeze
In a dangerous situation fighting can be helpful because if we fight the danger and win then there is no more danger. Even 'looking like' we are prepared to fight can make an opponent back down	It often makes sense to flee a dangerous situation in order to live another day. The phrase 'discretion is the better part of valor' captures this perfectly	In some situations it can make sense to freeze in the face of danger, especially to begin with. Some predators are only good at seeing movement, so it can make sense to freeze in case you haven't been spotted yet

We are designed to do these things automatically when we encounter threats. You can think of them as being part of our programming. Taken together, these are called the *fight-flight-freeze* response. It is not our fault when we respond in these ways, they are simply how we are designed.

This part of our programming that gets our body ready to deal with threat automatically causes changes in our body which prepare it for danger. The diagram below shows the changes that it causes, and the good reasons for each.

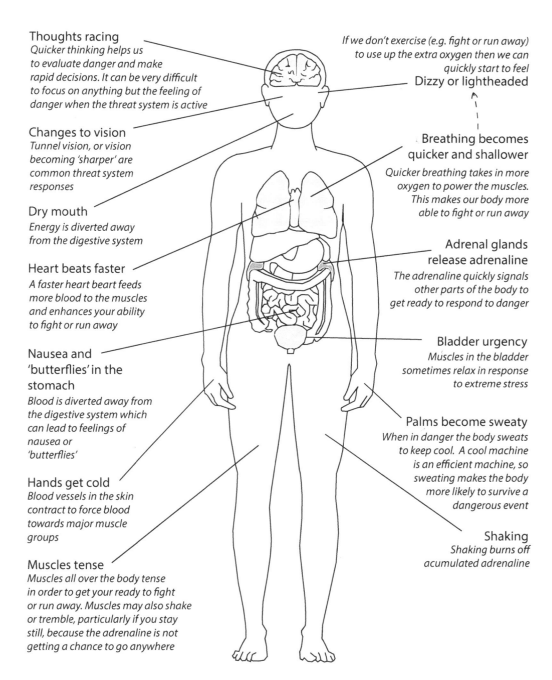

Thoughts racing
Quicker thinking helps us to evaluate danger and make rapid decisions. It can be very difficult to focus on anything but the feeling of danger when the threat system is active

Changes to vision
Tunnel vision, or vision becoming 'sharper' are common threat system responses

Dry mouth
Energy is diverted away from the digestive system

Heart beats faster
A faster heart beart feeds more blood to the muscles and enhances your ability to fight or run away

Nausea and 'butterflies' in the stomach
Blood is diverted away from the digestive system which can lead to feelings of nausea or 'butterflies'

Hands get cold
Blood vessels in the skin contract to force blood towards major muscle groups

Muscles tense
Muscles all over the body tense in order to get your ready to fight or run away. Muscles may also shake or tremble, particularly if you stay still, because the adrenaline is not getting a chance to go anywhere

If we don't exercise (e.g. fight or run away) to use up the extra oxygen then we can quickly start to feel
Dizzy or lightheaded

Breathing becomes quicker and shallower
Quicker breathing takes in more oxygen to power the muscles. This makes our body more able to fight or run away

Adrenal glands release adrenaline
The adrenaline quickly signals other parts of the body to get ready to respond to danger

Bladder urgency
Muscles in the bladder sometimes relax in response to extreme stress

Palms become sweaty
When in danger the body sweats to keep cool. A cool machine is an efficient machine, so sweating makes the body more likely to survive a dangerous event

Shaking
Shaking burns off acumulated adrenaline

Figure: The fight-flight-freeze response causes changes to happen throughout the body. Each of these changes happens for one reason – to help you to stay alive if there is a real threat. The fight-flight-freeze response is very sensitive and prefers to go off even if there is no real danger (false alarm) rather than miss a real danger.

Thoughts in panic

Human beings are thinking creatures. We think, plan, and fantasize all the time – we can't help it! We have thousands of thoughts per day and anything that happens to us can lead to a thought. Some thoughts are intentional, like when we deliberately try to remember where we left our keys, or decide what we want to eat. Other thoughts are automatic, like when we instinctively make a snap judgement (*"That's ugly"*), or when we judge other people (*"They're horrible"*), or ourselves (*"I'm useless"*).

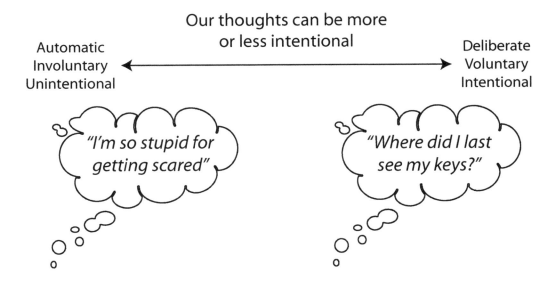

Figure: Our thoughts can be more or less intentional. Some thoughts are deliberate, whereas others are automatic.

Thinking is what makes human beings special. It means that we can make complicated decisions, plan ahead, solve difficult problems, live together in groups, and cooperate to help one another. But thinking come with costs too: we can worry, criticise ourselves, and dwell on our problems. The way we think affects the way we feel, and sometimes our thoughts can lead to us feeling overwhelmed.

Isn't it events (or other people) that bother me?

Our 'common sense' way of thinking about the world tells us that that it is events or situations that lead us to feel a certain way. For example:

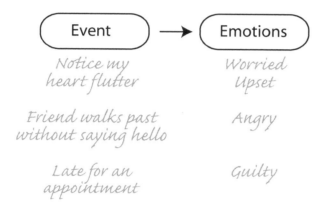

Event → Emotions

Notice my
heart flutter

Worried
Upset

Friend walks past
without saying hello

Angry

Late for an
appointment

Guilty

Figure: The 'common sense' view is that the way we feel is a direct result of the things we have experienced.

This is one of those times when common sense oversimplifies things. If events always led directly to feelings then everybody would always be affected in the same way by a particular event. We know that this is not the case though. Imagine being asked to sing in front of an audience – some people would be excited at the chance, whereas others would be horrified!

The CBT model says it is not events that bother us, instead it is the way that we interpret them (or the meaning that we give to them) that gives rise to our feelings. The way a person interprets any given situation will depend on their past experiences and prior beliefs. Look at the example below for three different ways of thinking about the same event.

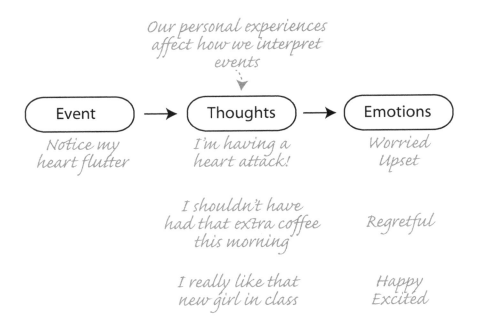

Figure: There are always different ways to interpret any given situation. We can choose how we think.

This doesn't just explain why people respond differently to the same event, it also shows us how we can feel different – by changing the way we think. The example above shows three different ways of interpreting the same situation. There is no 'right' way to think, and CBT is not just a matter of 'thinking positively', but it teaches us that the interpretation we instinctively leap to might not always be the most helpful one. CBT can teach you how to become more flexible in your thinking – flexibility gives you options regarding how you feel.

Catastrophic thoughts and anxious predictions

Different psychological problems are associated with different ways of thinking. For example, people who are depressed think a lot of negative thoughts and interpret things in a negative way. When we are depressed it can be difficult to remember the good things that have happened to us, so our thoughts are often very pessimistic or hopeless. Similarly, people who panic often think in a characteristic biased fashion. Three particularly unhelpful ways of thinking in panic are:

- Catastrophizing – blowing a situation our of all proportion and focusing on the worst possible outcome – e.g. Ted's boss asks him to do a job and Ted thinks *"I don't know how to do it, I'll mess it up and be fired"*

- Fortune telling – making anxious predictions about what is likely to happen in the future. Often involves chaining together lots of anxious predictions – e.g. *"He doesn't like me. He'll tell all his friends I'm a loser. I'll be an outcast"*

- Jumping to conclusions – adding 2 and 2 and coming up with 5 – e.g. *"My friend didn't phone me up today, that must mean they've given up on me"*

Have you ever thought in any of these ways? When people panic they make anxious predictions about what is happening to them, and about what they think will happen to them in the future. Because the way we think affects the way we feel these thoughts can have a dramatic effect upon our emotions.

Mistaken thoughts in panic

It is possible to panic about anything, but some anxious predictions appear more frequently than others. Listed below are some common myths in panic disorder. Notice how many of them are anxious predictions about what might happen in the future.

"I'm going to have a heart attack"

A common worry in panic is interpreting a racing heartbeat or palpitations as believing that you are about to have a heart attack. This is a catastrophic interpretation of that set of body sensations. However, the overlap between the symptoms of a panic attack and symptoms of a heart attack is only superficial – mainly breathlessness. Really, the major symptoms of each are quite different. Heart attacks are associated with chest pain and breathlessness; palpitations are less common.

One helpful piece of information about heart attacks is that they get worse with exertion – this is quite different from panic attacks which often feel a little better if we exercise. One way of telling for sure is to have an echocardiogram (EKG) recording of the heart activity, which will show evidence of heart disease. It is quite common for people with panic to have had an EKG and been told that their symptoms were due to anxiety. If you have had an EKG and your doctor has ruled out heart disease then you can safely assume that your panic attacks will not cause a heart attack.

"I'm going to faint"

Although a feeling of lightheadedness is common in panic it is not the same as the feeling of fainting, and does not mean that you are going to faint. People with panic often make the mistake of thinking that feeling dizzy and lightheaded means you are about to faint. In fact, fainting is associated with low blood pressure, whereas in a state of anxiety or panic blood pressure tends to be higher than normal. This makes it quite difficult to faint when we are anxious.

"I'm going to suffocate"

This is similar to the *"I'm going to faint"* belief, and is equally mistaken. Remember that people can breathe perfectly safely and happily in a sauna or steam room, or in a crowded environment like a music concert. It would take being in a very extreme environment for you to actually run out of air. If anything, people who have panic attacks are overbreathing (hyperventilating) which means they are taking in too much air. This hyperventilation causes a temporary change in the acidity of the blood which can lead to feeling uncomfortable – but it is not dangerous. Anxious breathing is often very tense and high up in the chest taking quick shallow breaths. The solution is to breathe more slowly, and lower down in the belly.

"I'm going to lose control and run amok"

Fear of losing control is very worry common in panic. Sometimes people have the idea that they will act unpredictably by shouting insults, acting wildly, or embarrassing themselves.

When people are panicking their fight-flight-freeze programming becomes active. In this state the focus of attention narrows to pay more attention to opportunities to feel safe – typically by looking for ways out of the anxiety provoking situation. Your responses in fight-flight-freeze mode are actually quite predictable and therefore 'in control'. The typical order of action would be to freeze initially to assess options, then try to run away, and only to become irritable or aggressive if there were no other options.

"I'm going to go insane"

Going insane or losing your mind is sometimes the biggest worry in people who panic. Many people who panic confuse the physical symptoms of fear with going insane. When we think of 'going insane' we often think of people with psychosis who hear voices (hallucinations) or believe in strange things that aren't true (delusions). Psychosis is a very different disorder from panic. Panic attacks are much more common than psychosis, and are typically a more likely explanation for what you are feeling. Although it is scary nobody has ever gone insane from fear. It is important to remember that fear and the accompanying body sensations are just a normal response to perceived danger.

Behaviors in panic

The fight-flight-freeze response gets us ready to act when we perceive danger. Human beings are designed to behave automatically when they encounter danger. In a way this is part of our programming. It is not our fault when we respond by freezing, running away of becoming aggressive when we are scared: this is simply how we are designed. In very frightening situations it is typically only people with specialist training and lots of practise, for example soldiers or emergency workers, who can easily overcome these automatic behaviors.

When psychologists treat panic they tend to be most interested in three types of behaviors: escape, avoidance, and safety behaviors. These are common responses when we perceive danger, but they are not always helpful.

Escape

Escaping from situations which make us afraid is the 'flight' part of the fight-flight-freeze system. 'Taking flight' or escaping from threatening situations is an evolved automatic response to danger. In situations where there is genuine danger escaping is a very sensible option: it means that we live to fight another day. The problem in panic is that the perception of danger is based on a mistaken belief – the situations in which we panic are not truly dangerous. Our fight-flight-freeze system isn't very clever though, and relies on a 'better safe than sorry' approach: it would always prefer to escape unnecessarily than to miss a real danger. This is problematic for a number of reasons. Firstly, if we spend a lot of time 'escaping' from situations that are not truly dangerous we waste a lot of time and nervous energy. Secondly, and more importantly, escaping means that we never get to find out how dangerous that situation truly is and whether we could have coped after all.

Avoidance

It is natural to want to avoid threat or pain. Everyone does this, and used in the right amount avoidance is a helpful strategy for managing our emotions. For example, I might avoid my boss when I haven't done something she has asked me to do, or avoid tidying up when I feel tired. However, avoidance can become problematic when it is our only strategy for managing emotions, or when it is a strategy that we call on too often. For example, it is definitely a problem if I always make a habit of avoiding my boss, or if I never tidy up.

Avoidance is powerful because the relief we can get from avoiding something (*"phew, that was close"*) is an extremely strong positive feeling. Our brain interprets relief as *"that was a good choice, do that again in the future"*. In panic this means that we quickly come to rely on avoidance too strongly, which can affect how confident we feel in managing similar situations in the future.

Safety behaviors

Safety behaviors are things that we do to keep ourselves safe from a feared catastrophe. Escape and avoidance are very obvious types of safety behaviors. If we are faced with a situation that we can't escape or avoid we often resort to using more subtle types of safety behaviors, for example:

- Carrying a bottle of water to prevent the feared danger of my throat closing up

- Not making eye contact with the teacher in case I'm picked on to give an answer and I embarrass myself

- Worry that I'm going to collapse in the supermarket so hold on tightly to the trolley

- Sitting at the back of a theatre, or on an aisle, in case I need to escape

Safety behaviors are driven by our beliefs. If I have a belief that I'm too hot and going to faint then my safety behaviors will be focused on preventing that from happening, or limiting how bad the consequences would be if the worst did happen: perhaps by cooling down (prevention) or sitting down (limiting catastrophic consequences).

Feared catastrophe	Safety behavior
"My throat will close up and I won't be able to breathe"	Carry a bottle of water
"A stranger will start a fight if I look at them"	Not make eye contact
"I'm going to collapse"	Hold on tightly to the trolley in the super-market
"I'll be trapped and go mad"	Sit at the back or on an aisle for an easy escape

Safety behaviors are a key part of what keeps panic disorder going. In the short term they often feel good (because they bring relief or make us feel safe) but in the long term they can have unhelpful consequences such as preventing us from learning about how dangerous a situation really is, or what we are truly able to manage.

How does this all add up to a panic attack?

Panic attacks involve thoughts, emotions, body sensations and behaviors. These interact in stages to result in a panic attack.

Stage 1

Panic attacks start with a trigger. We may or may not be aware of what this is – sometimes panic feels like it comes 'out of the blue' Sometimes the trigger is a place or situation that makes us anxious (perhaps a place where we have panicked before), or it could be something internal like a feeling in our body (for example we might notice that our heart is beating faster than normal).

Stage 2

It is natural to think about whatever we are experiencing. If we think in very negative ways about what we are experiencing, or make anxious predictions about what we expect to experience, it leads to anxiety. Important 'thinking errors' in panic are: catastrophizing, 'fortune telling' and jumping to conclusions.

Stage 3

These negative interpretations (thoughts about our experience) lead to the emotion of fear or anxiety, and set off the fight-flight-freeze response. The body then tries to help and prepares itself for danger by increasing processes like heart rate, breathing, and sweating.

Stage 4

These changes in body sensation are noticed and misinterpreted (thoughts) as being dangerous – e.g. *"My heart is racing – that must mean that I'm going to have a heart attack"*. This leads to more fear and anxiety.

Stage 5

A vicious circle has been created. Irrespective of how the panic started, anxious thoughts are leading to anxious emotions, which lead to anxious body sensations and more anxious thoughts about the body sensations and their consequences. Panic ramps up very quickly because of this feedback loop, just like the feedback noise when you hold a microphone too close to a speaker.

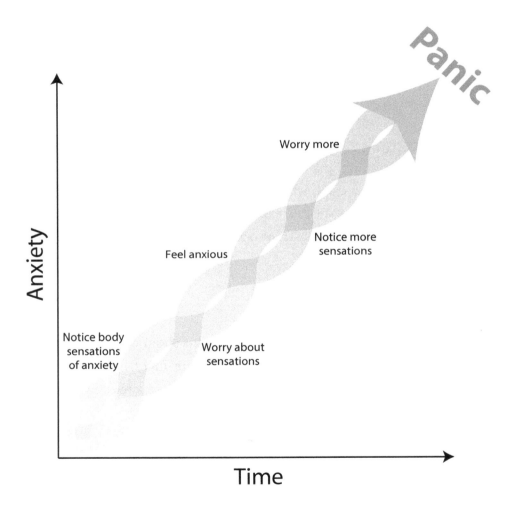

Figure: Anxious thoughts can spiral, creating more anxiety, and more anxious body sensations. If it is not stopped it can become panic.

We can show this process in a different way to see how it ends up in a vicious cycle that goes round and around. Panic attacks can build up from a small sensation to quickly feel overwhelming.

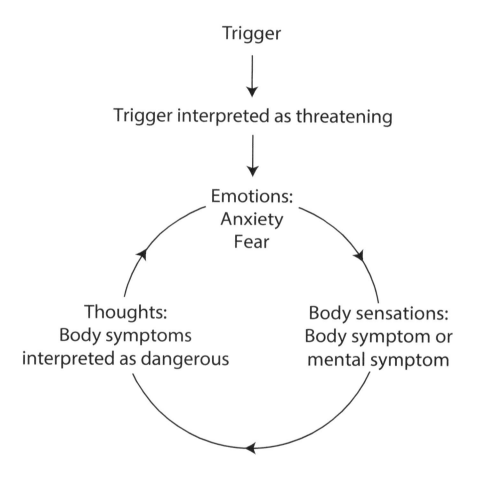

Figure: Another way of showing a panic attack is with a 'vicious circle'. Anxious thoughts, feelings, and body sensations feed into each other and explain why panic attacks quickly increase in intensity.

Why do I keep getting panic attacks?

So now we understand how an individual panic attack happens. But panic disorder is not just about having single panic attacks, it also involves worrying about panic attacks, and taking steps to avoid having more of them in the future. Why does panic continue to be distressing? An example from Ted's life can illustrate how panic persists.

After he had experienced a couple of panic attacks Ted quickly started to do things to try and prevent any more from happening. These are called 'safety behaviors' – things that we do to try to feel safe. In Ted's case he:

- Stopped going to places where he had panicked before in case it happened again

- Stopped exercising in case he got out of breath again

- Would take deep breaths to check that his lungs were working properly

- Would pay a lot of attention to whether his breathing was ok in case he became breathless again

All of these safety behaviors made a lot of sense to Ted, and they made him feel a bit safer whilst he was doing them. Unfortunately, what we know about panic tells us that although these safety behaviors can make us feel better in the short term, they make us more likely to experience panic in the future. A helpful way to think about this is to consider the intended and unintended consequences of an action.

Action	Intended consequence	Unintended consequence
Avoid the place where panic has happened in the past	• Avoid what we think is going to be a catastrophe • Avoid the fear that this place triggers • Short term feeling of relief	• Don't get to learn how dangerous that place truly is • List of 'safe places' to go gets smaller and smaller
Try to avoid a particular body sensation	• Avoid what we think is going to be a catastrophe • Short term feeling of relief	• Always on the look-out for particular body sensations • Watching out for particular body sensations can actually make them more likely to happen • Possibility for anxiety is with you wherever you go: you can't escape your own body!
Use safety behaviors to prevent feared catastrophes	• Avoid what we think is going to be a catastrophe. • Short term feeling of relief	• Don't get to learn how dangerous the situation really is • Feel very anxious if preferred safety behaviour isn't possible or available • Focusing your attention internally means you are more likely to notice all sorts of body sensations which might trigger further panic

It seems that our actions, however well-intentioned, often result in unintended consequences. Some of these consequences have important implications for our experience of panic.

Problems of escape, avoidance, and safety behaviors

Avoiding situations which have been associated with panic makes some places a 'no go' area and shrinks our lives

It is common sense to avoid real dangers. If we are mugged in a dark alley one night, it is sensible not to want to go back to the same alley the next night. However, the fear in panic is about catastrophes that *might* happen (anxious predictions) rather than about what has happened. The bodily sensations of panic are uncomfortable but they are not truly dangerous. If we start to avoid everywhere we have panicked then our world quickly starts shrinking, as there are fewer and fewer places we feel that we can go safely. This quickly affects our sense of competence, and it is easy to start thinking we are incapable.

Avoiding the bodily or mental symptoms of panic means that you don't get a chance to learn how dangerous they really are

When he panicked Ted was worried that he wouldn't be able to breathe and that he might suffocate. He had a clear image in his mind of himself gasping for breath. In order to avoid this feared catastrophe it made sense to him to avoid anything which could affect his breathing. He stopped exercising and avoided any form of physical exertion. Unfortunately for Ted this meant that he never got to find out that his symptom of a tight chest was just due to anxiety – part of the fight-flight-freeze response – and was not dangerous at all. All of his safety behaviors were keeping him 'safe' from a threat that wasn't really there! Worse, not doing any exercise was a genuine danger to his health.

Safety behaviors make us more likely to pay attention to the bodily symptoms of panic

One of Ted's safety behaviors was to always be on the lookout for signs of shortness of breath. Other people with panic might pay attention to whether their heart is racing, or whether they are feeling strange. With real threats it is a sensible strategy to stay on the lookout for signs of danger – you wouldn't cross the road without looking! But in panic, where none of the uncomfortable body sensations are truly dangerous, staying on the lookout for these sensations is a problem because it just makes us more likely to notice them. And if someone with panic notices a body or mental symptom they are concerned about then they are likely to have panicky thoughts about it, which leads to anxiety, which leads to more symptoms and panicky thoughts, and then another panic attack has started. A process that started out as well-intentioned (look out for 'danger') ends up causing the feelings it is trying to prevent.

Part 3

What can I do about my panic?

Overcoming panic disorder with self-help

Cognitive behavioral therapy (CBT) is a very effective treatment for panic. The information and exercises in this self-help book are the same as those you would learn about and practice if you had sessions of CBT for panic face-to-face with a psychologist.

As effective as CBT is, just reading this self-help book is not enough on its own. You will also need to dedicate time to practising the exercises. It is best to repeat each of the exercises until you have mastered them. A rough guide might be to spend a week or so practising each of the steps outlined in the rest of this book, although some of the longer sections may require more time for you to master.

Remember that the path to progress is rarely smooth and it is possible that you will have some setbacks along the way. If this happens don't give up! Remind yourself why you want to overcome your panic, and what you stand to gain from facing your fears.

Step 1: How much do you know about panic?

The first step in overcoming panic is really understanding what it is all about. Take the panic quiz below to see what you remember from parts 1 and 2 of this book.

	True	False
Panic symptoms are dangerous		✓
People have gone mad from panic attacks		✓
Anxious predictions can make panic worse	✓	
Having panic means that I am likely to become severely mentally ill		✓
Panic symptoms are my body's way of protecting me from danger	✓	
Anxiety always means there is danger		✓
Panic is maintained by mistaken beliefs	✓	
If I avoid triggers for my panic I won't have any more panic attacks		✓
I can stop panic attacks by avoiding the places that cause them		✓
The way I think affects the anxiety I feel	✓	

The answers are on the next page. How many did you get right? If any of the answers didn't seem straightforward go back and read part 2 again.

Answers for quiz on previous page: F, F, T, F, T, F, T, F, F, T

Step 2: Monitoring your panic

In order to overcome your panic first you need to know all about it. Using CBT this means learning when your panic occurs and what triggers it (situation) understanding how panic feels in your body (emotions and body sensations) and noticing what goes through your mind when you panic (thoughts). Once you understand how all of these parts fit together you will be able to take steps to put right any difficulties.

The best way to understand your panic is to develop the habit of keeping a record. Good records are important because otherwise our memories of what has happened can easily be biased or distorted by the strong emotions that panic brings. Having accurate records helps us begin to bring the emotions under control. It is recommended that you keep records of your panic attacks for at least a week before you progress to the next steps in this book.

Recording your panic attacks

Use the *panic attack record* form whenever you have panic attacks, and when you have 'near misses' where you felt very anxious but avoided having a full panic attack. Try to record the details as soon as possible after the panic attack. Don't wait until the end of the day – psychologists have found that you are much more likely to remember the important details if you complete it soon after the event. Make sure that you are prepared by carrying spare copies of the record form with you. There are blank forms at the back of this book and you can download additional forms from the Psychology Tools website (http://psychologytools.com).

There is an example of Ted's completed panic attack record on the next page.

Panic Attack Record

Date & Time	Fear rating (0-100%)
Tuesday 5th March at 11:00am	*90%*

Situation Where were you? Who were you with?	Trigger What do you think caused your panic to start at that moment?
At the checkout of the supermarket *On my own*	*Too many people around me*

Symptoms

- ☑ Heart pounding, racing, or palpitations
- ☑ Sweating
- ☐ Trembling or shaking
- ☑ Shortness of breath
- ☐ Feeling of choking
- ☐ Chest pain or discomfort
- ☐ Nausea or stomach distress
- ☐ Dizziness, lightheadedness, or feeling faint
- ☑ Chills or hot flushes
- ☐ Numbness or tingling
- ☑ Feelings of unreality
- ☑ Fear of losing control or going crazy
- ☐ Fear of dying

Thoughts (or images)
What was going through your mind?
What were you predicting would happen?

I can't cope with this. I'm going to embarrass myself

Coping strategy
What did you do to cope?
What action did you take that made you feel better?

Pretended I'd forgotten something then went to a quiet part of the store and
waited there until there was less of a queue at the checkout

Figure: Ted's panic attack record form.

How to complete a panic attack record

The panic attack record form guides you to record key information about a panic attack. Let's look at what details you need to record:

- The date & time

- Your fear rating – How severe was this panic attack? Rate your fear and anxiety from 0% (no fear at all, completely calm) to 100% (total fear & panic)

- The situation – Record where you were, who were you with, and what you were doing just before the panic started

- The trigger – Think about what might have triggered your panic in that moment. What was going on around you that you found anxiety-pro voking? Did you notice any body sensations that worried you? Did you have any panicky thoughts just before the anxiety got worse?

- Symptoms – Record the symptoms you noticed in your body and mind. Select them from the list, or make notes about additional ones if they are not listed

- Thoughts – Our thoughts and beliefs are a key part of panic. Record what you were thinking just before the panic started, and during the panic attack. Good questions to ask yourself include *"What was going through my mind?"*, *"What was I worried might happen?"*, *"Did I notice any images in my mind?"*, *"Was I making any predictions about the future?"*

- Coping – We always try to cope as best we can with any strong emotions. What did you do to cope with this panic attack? What action did you take that led you to feel better?

On the next page is a blank panic attack record form. Think back to the last panic attack you had (or the first panic attack you ever had) and complete the form now. Make sure to record details of any panic attacks you have from now on panic attack record forms. You will need some extra forms: either cut out some of the blank copies of the panic attack record from the back of this book, or print some out from Psychology Tools (http://psychologytools.com).

Panic Attack Record

Date & Time	Fear rating (0-100%)

Situation	Trigger
Where were you?	What do you think caused your
Who were you with?	panic to start at that moment?

Symptoms

- ☐ Heart pounding, racing, or palpitations
- ☐ Sweating
- ☐ Trembling or shaking
- ☐ Shortness of breath
- ☐ Feeling of choking
- ☐ Chest pain or discomfort
- ☐ Nausea or stomach distress
- ☐ Dizziness, lightheadedness, or feeling faint
- ☐ Chills or hot flushes
- ☐ Numbness or tingling
- ☐ Feelings of unreality
- ☐ Fear of losing control or going crazy
- ☐ Fear of dying

Thoughts (or images)
What was going through your mind?
What were you predicting would happen?

Coping strategy
What did you do to cope?
What action did you take that made you feel better?

Figure: Panic attack record form. You will find blank copies at the back of this book, and you can download more forms from Psychology Tools (http://psychologytools.com)

Recording your anxiety and worry

Remember that while panic attacks are about sudden bursts of fear, panic disorder is characterised by more general anxiety throughout the day. People with panic disorder often worry about whether another panic attack will occur and have higher than usual levels of anxiety.

A helpful way to record your progress is to monitor your anxiety and worry over time. An example of Ted's 'panic daily mood record' is on the next page. Keep a copy of this form by your bedside and use it to record your average anxiety and worry at the end of each day. There are blank copies at the back of this book, and you can download and print more from Psychology Tools (http://psychologytools.com).

Panic Daily Mood Record

Record your mood every day so that you can monitor your progress. At the end of each week record your average scores on the panic attack progress record form.

Day / Date	Anxiety (0-100%) How anxious were you today?	Worry About Panic (0-100%) How much did you worry about having another panic attack?
Week 1		
Monday 1st	80%	90%
Tuesday 2nd	50%	60%
Wednesday 3rd	20%	10%
Thursday 4th	90%	80%
Friday 5th	80%	60%
Saturday 6th	20%	40%
Sunday 7th	40%	60%
Week 2		
Monday 8th	60%	90%
Tuesday 9th	60%	80%
Wednesday 10th	70%	90%
Thursday 11th	40%	10%
Friday 12th	40%	10%
Saturday 13th	50%	20%
Sunday 14th	20%	10%
Week 3		
Monday 15th	50%	50%
Tuesday 16th	20%	10%
Wednesday 17th	20%	10%
Thursday 18th	20%	10%
Friday 19th	50%	40%
Saturday 20th	40%	10%
Sunday 21st	30%	10%
Week 4		
Monday 22nd	40%	30%
Tuesday 23rd	30%	40%
Wednesday 24th	10%	40%
Thursday 25th	30%	10%
Friday 26th	10%	10%
Saturday 27th	10%	10%
Sunday 28th	10%	10%

Figure: Ted's panic daily mood record. You will find blank copies at the back of the book, and you can download more forms from Psychology Tools (http://psychologytools.com)

Monitor your progress

A good way to stay motivated to overcome your panic is to keep a visual record of your progress. At the end of each week count the number of panic attacks you had that week (from your panic attack record forms), the average anxiety you felt (from your panic daily mood record), and the average worry you felt about panic (from your panic daily mood record). Keep these charts somewhere visible so that you are reminded of the progress that you are making. An example of Ted's panic attack progress record is on the next page. There are blank copies at the back of this book, and you can download and print more from Psychology Tools (http://psychologytools.com).

Panic Attack Progress Record

Regularly and accurately recording how you feel is very important in therapy.
You should make the habit of doing it every day in order to obtain the most benefit.

Recording your symptoms every day:
✓ Gives you more accurate information compared to just asking yourself *"how have I been feeling lately?"*
✓ Allows you to evaluate your progress over time

The forms on the following pages allow you to record details of any panic attacks you have, and your daily moods, for a month. You should complete a separate form for every panic attack. If you need more forms you can download them from PsychologyTools

Use the graphs below to record your progress at the end of each week.

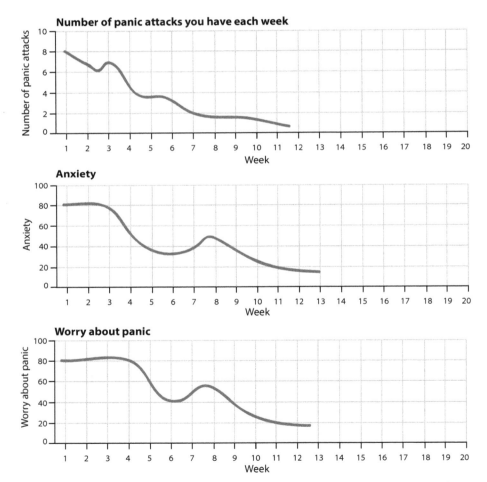

Figure: Ted's panic attack progress record. Use these at the end of every week to record your progress. You will find blank copies at the back of the book, and you can download more forms from Psychology Tools (http://psychologytools.com)

Step 3: The parts of your panic

Do you remember the CBT model of panic from part 2? Panic is a vicious cycle. The cycle often starts when you notice a feeling of anxiety and pay attention to it. Whenever we pay attention to something we notice more details about it (You can test this quickly right now: pay attention to how your feet feel right now. Are they warm or cold? Dry or sweaty? What do you notice? Were you aware of all these sensations five minutes ago?). In panic, when we pay attention to a feeling of anxiety we notice body sensations associated with it. If these body sensations are misinterpreted as signs of danger then we feel even more anxious. The anxiety leads to more body sensations and so this starts the cycle all over again.

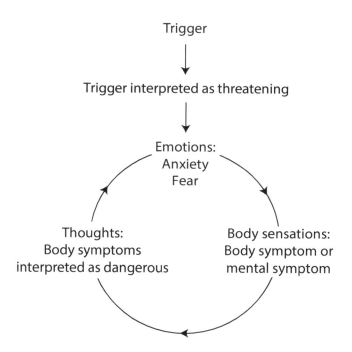

Figure: A vicious cycle of panic. Anxious thoughts and feelings feed into each other and panic builds up very quickly.

Once a panic attack has started we take actions to make the awful feelings go away. These behaviors often work in the short term, but are typically not effective in the long term at helping to stop you from having further panic attacks. So the ingredients of panic are: emotions, body sensations, thoughts and behaviors. Let's examine them in more detail.

Emotions in panic

People use different words to describe the emotions in panic – anxious, afraid, terrified, scared – but really they mean the same thing. These are all 'threat' emotions. They are what we feel when we sense danger. These threat emotions are designed to be highly motivating and hard to ignore – their purpose is to encourage you to take action to deal with the 'danger'. In the CBT model our emotions don't exist in isolation – they are linked to our body sensations, our thoughts, and our behaviors or actions.

Use the space below to record the emotions you feel during a panic attack. Emotional reactions can normally be described using single words (e.g. sad, angry, scared).

Emotions I feel during a panic attack

Body sensations in panic

Any emotion is accompanied by particular body sensations: when we are feeling contented our bodies relax, when we are embarrassed our bodies blush, and when we are feeling angry our bodies become tense. Fear and anxiety are no exception and are accompanied by their own set of body sensations. In the previous chapter you were encouraged to record the physical sensations you experience when you have a panic attack. The following body reactions are very typical:

- Heart pounding, racing, or palpitations
- Sweating
- Trembling or shaking
- Shortness of breath
- Feeling of choking
- Chest pain or discomfort
- Nausea or stomach distress
- Dizziness, lightheadedness, or feeling faint
- Chills or hot flushes
- Numbness or tingling
- Feelings of unreality
- Fear of losing control or going crazy
- Fear of dying

You might experience a typical set of body sensations every time you have a panic attack, or your body sensations might vary each time. Remember that all of the body sensations listed above are by-products of your fight-flight-freeze system being activated. None of them are dangerous, they are just a natural consequence of your body's internal safety system being activated.

Use the space below to record the body sensations you experience during a panic attack.

Body sensations I am aware of during a panic attack

Thoughts in panic

Thoughts are the most important part of panic because the way we think affects the way we feel. We are thinking creatures and always try to make sense of whatever we are experiencing – panic attacks are no exception. The typical thoughts in panic all share a common theme: concern about threats to our physical or mental well-being. Common thoughts about threat in panic include:

Fear of dying

The feelings of panic are so strong that some people fear that something terrible is going to happen and that they might die. Even though panic is harmless these thoughts can still feel overwhelming. These kind of panic thoughts might happen anywhere.

Fear of embarrassment

Some people with panic worry about making a fool of themselves. It is threatening to worry that other people might think badly of us – that we are silly or weak for example. This fear of embarrassment might be stronger in some situations, such as at work, and weaker in other situations, such as when you are with close friends.

Fear of losing control

Some people with panic worry that they will 'go crazy' or 'run amok', and might be concerned about hurting other people. Sometimes they might have a picture in their mind of what 'losing control' would look like. Feelings of panic are completely normal, and are just your body's way of keeping you safe from danger. If anything, people who are panicking are normally very 'in control' - their focus on escaping or making the feelings stop are good examples of this 'in control' behavior.

Fear of being unable to escape

People with panic sometimes worry that they are trapped or might not be able to escape from a fearful situation. Crowded places such as cinemas, restaurants, or public transport might trigger this kind of panic. This fear is often less intense in places such as at home which are perceived as 'safe'.

Fear of not being able to get help

Most of us feel safer when we have help to hand. A common worry in panic is the thought that *"I won't be able to get help if something terrible happens"*. People who panic often take precautions to prevent the worst from happening. This might mean having someone with us, not travelling too far from somewhere 'safe', or keeping a mobile phone to hand in order to call for help.

Use the space below to record the thoughts you typically experience during a panic attack. These might include worries, fear, or anxious predictions. Try to be as specific as you can.

Thoughts I have during a panic attack

Behaviors, actions, and responses in panic

The purpose of our feelings and body sensations is to make us want to act. It is as though feelings have been designed so that we cannot ignore them. Different emotions are designed to make us want to do different things, for example:

- Happiness – makes us want to do more of whatever we are doing

- Contentment – makes us want to stay exactly as we are

- Guilt – makes us want to repair any damage we might have caused

- Anger – makes us want to put right the injustice that has wronged us

Fear and anxiety encourage us to act to make ourselves safe from danger. We have evolved automatic fight-flight-freeze responses to deal with certain types of life-threatening danger. The problem in panic is that the fight-flight-freeze response is too sensitive – it is going off inappropriately and making us act when we don't need to. One problem of this is that although our natural responses to keep ourselves safe, like escaping or avoiding, can make us feel good in the short-term they often come with unhelpful consequences that make panic attacks more likely in the future.

Natural response 1: escape from the situation which feels dangerous

Often the best way to cope with something truly dangerous is to get away from it. Imagine if a dangerous animal were to suddenly appear where you are now – the best way to survive would be to escape! When we are feeling afraid it is normal to want to escape from the source of danger. 'Taking flight' is all about escaping.

Whenever we escape from a situation we think is dangerous we can feel a tremendous sense of relief. Relief feels good, and we are likely to take similar actions in the future because that feeling of relief is preferable to feelings of anxiety. However, while relief feels good in the short term, one unintended consequence of always escaping from situations we fear is that we never get to find out how dangerous that situation truly is. In panic, where we catastrophize and magnify the dangers, this means that escaping prevents us from facing and overcoming our fears.

Intended short-term consequences of escape	Unintended long-term consequences of escape
• Escape and feel immediate relief	• Never get to find out how dangerous the situation really is • Anxiety is prolonged • Don't get to overcome our fears • Start to feel that we are incapable

Natural response 2: avoid situations which make us anxious

It also makes sense to want to avoid situations that have hurt or scared us. A simple example is burning our hand on a hot stove – if we do it once we take care to avoid doing so again. Avoidance works for true dangers like hot stoves and dangerous animals, but in panic we are really trying to avoid an unpleasant body feeling. And because feelings come from inside us, and are made worse by how we think about them, our normal strategies like avoidance are not very effective.

Intended short-term consequences of avoidance	Unintended long-term consequences of avoidance
• Don't have to face a fear • Feeling of relief from having 'dodged a bullet'	• Don't get to find out how dangerous the situation really is • Can waste effort avoiding situations that you would have been able to cope with • Anxiety is prolonged • Can feel incapable of doing 'normal' things

Natural response 3: safety behaviors

When we feel threatened but cannot escape or avoid it is common to resort to using safety-seeking behaviors. Safety behaviors are things we do that we think will prevent a catastrophe. Some typical safety behaviors in panic include:

- Carrying a bottle of water to prevent my throat from closing up

- Holding on for support in case I fall and embarrass myself

- Sitting near an exit for an easy escape in case I feel trapped

- Making excuses early to make a later escape seem more plausible in case I need to leave suddenly

Intended short-term consequences of safety behaviors	Unintended long-term consequences of safety behaviors
• Feeling of safety and reassurance	• They prevent us from facing our fears • They prevent us from learning about our true abilities to cope

Natural response 4: fight

If we are feeling feelings of fear and anxiety but we can't escape it is natural to feel more short-tempered or irritable. 'Fight' is part of the fight-flight-freeze response. For some people fight often comes at the end, after other strategies have failed. Others find that they reach 'fight' much more quickly.

Intended short-term consequences of becoming irritable or angry	Unintended long-term consequences becoming irritable or angry
• What we say or do becomes more forceful and may help us to escape or avoid	• Exacerbates the problems of the other coping behaviors • Can harm our relationships

Use the space below to record the things you do to cope when you have a panic attack. Consider 'big' actions like escaping, and more subtle actions too.

My behaviors or actions when I have a panic attack

Step 4: Making sense of your panic

Let's put together everything we have learned so far. Panic is to do with the emotions of feeling afraid, anxious, or scared. Our bodies react automatically to these signs of danger and we become more aware of bodily symptoms. We think about what we are experiencing, and our thoughts can make the danger seem more severe than it really is. The feeling of fear gets stronger. We take action to make ourselves feel better in the short-term, but our behaviors come with unintended consequences. These thoughts, feelings, body sensations and actions create a vicious cycle where panic can quickly ramp up.

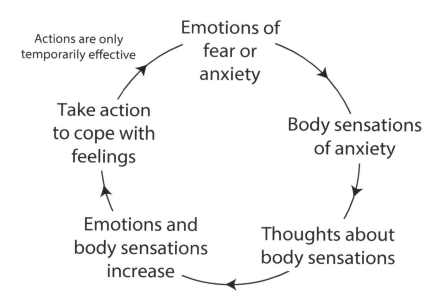

Figure: A vicious cycle of panic. Anxious feelings, body sensations, thoughts, and behaviors feed into each other.

Understanding your panic

Now we know how panic works in general it is worth thinking about some specific examples. A diagram of Ted's panic is on the next page.

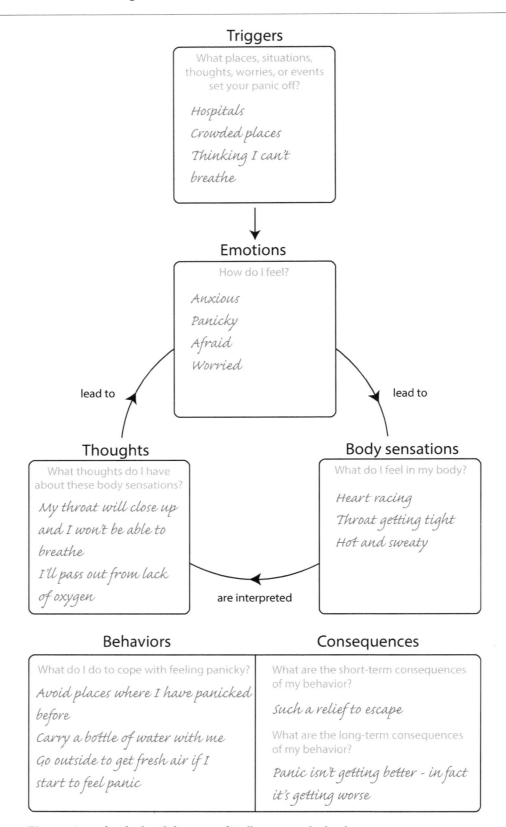

Triggers

What places, situations, thoughts, worries, or events set your panic off?

Hospitals

Crowded places

Thinking I can't breathe

Emotions

How do I feel?

Anxious

Panicky

Afraid

Worried

lead to

lead to

Thoughts

What thoughts do I have about these body sensations?

My throat will close up and I won't be able to breathe

I'll pass out from lack of oxygen

Body sensations

What do I feel in my body?

Heart racing

Throat getting tight

Hot and sweaty

are interpreted

Behaviors

What do I do to cope with feeling panicky?

Avoid places where I have panicked before

Carry a bottle of water with me

Go outside to get fresh air if I start to feel panic

Consequences

What are the short-term consequences of my behavior?

Such a relief to escape

What are the long-term consequences of my behavior?

Panic isn't getting better - in fact it's getting worse

Figure: An individualized diagram of Ted's panic and what keeps it going

Now let's consider how your panic works. Think about the answers to the following questions and complete the personalizable panic vicious cycle on the next page.

- What tends to trigger your panic? Is it an emotion, a body sensation, or a thought? This tells you where on the vicious cycle you start.

- What emotions do you feel?

- What kinds of body sensations do you experience? What happens to these over time?

- What thoughts do you have during your panic attack? What does your anxious mind predict will happen? What do you fear is going to happen?

- What how do you feel when you think these worrying thoughts?

- What do you do to cope? If you can't escape from a situation what do you do to manage in the situation? How does this make you feel in the short-term? Does it stop the panic you feel in the long-term?

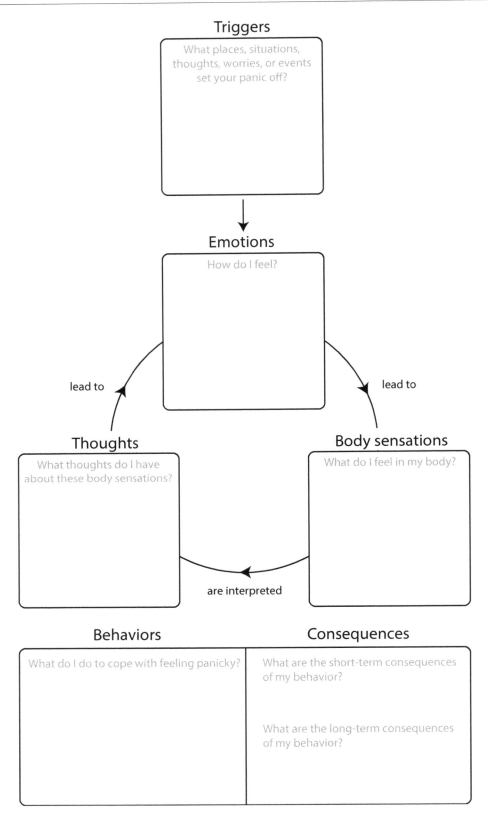

Figure: An individualized panic diagram

Breaking the vicious cycle

The great thing about vicious cycles is that they can be broken. Like a chain they are made up of links, but they are only as strong as the weakest link. If any link in the chain is broken then it all falls apart. The rest of this book will help you to target different links in the chain. You will learn some exercises to control your body sensations, learn how to work with your anxious thoughts, and learn different ways you can react to overcome your panic.

Step 5: Breathing to calm the body sensations of panic

The way we breathe is closely linked to the way we feel. When we are calm and relaxed our breathing is slow and deep, but when we are afraid or anxious our breathing becomes quicker and shallower. This happens because our breathing is linked automatically to our fight-flight-freeze response. When our body's threat detection system senses danger it sends signals to prepare the body for running away or fighting. One effect of this is that the threat system speeds up our breathing rate to take in more oxygen. In a truly dangerous situation this is helpful because the muscles have more 'fuel' in case they are needed to help you with fighting or running away from a danger. In a panic attack, where our perception of danger is caused by a misinterpretation of unwanted body sensations, this extra readiness for danger is unnecessary, unhelpful, and uncomfortable. We can reduce the uncomfortable feelings of panic by deliberately changing the way we breathe.

For people who panic breathing properly is important for two reasons. The first is that practising relaxed breathing (and other relaxation techniques) can help you to become calmer generally. This is helpful because the lower your general level of stress the less likely you are to experience a panic attack in the first place. The second reason why breathing properly is important is because your breathing will change during a panic attack. Using a relaxed breathing technique to breathe properly reverses this change and sends a message to the body that there is no danger and no need to panic. This can stop the vicious cycle of panic.

Types of breathing

Before learning relaxed breathing it is helpful to know about how our breathing works.

Normal breathing

When we breathe we take in oxygen (O_2) to be used by the body. As the body uses oxygen it creates carbon dioxide (CO_2), a waste product that we breathe out. When we are breathing normally the levels of oxygen and carbon dioxide are balanced.

Exercise breathing

Our breathing rate increases during exercise to take in more oxygen. The body uses the extra oxygen to fuel the muscles as they do extra work and so produces more carbon dioxide. The increased breathing rate leads to more carbon dioxide being expelled. Even though there are increased levels of oxygen and carbon dioxide the balance is maintained.

Panic breathing

When we are anxious our breathing rate increases: we take in more oxygen and breathe out more carbon dioxide than usual. However, because the body is not working any harder than normal it is not using up any extra oxygen, and so it is not producing any extra carbon dioxide. Because carbon dioxide is being expelled faster than it is being produced its concentration in the blood goes down. This leads to a temporary change in the pH of the blood called respiratory alkalosis. The change in CO_2 blood concentration can lead us to feel unpleasantly light-headed, tingly in our fingers and toes, clammy, and sweaty.

Normal breathing

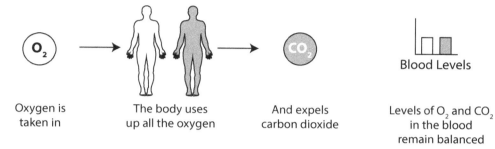

Oxygen is taken in | The body uses up all the oxygen | And expels carbon dioxide | Levels of O_2 and CO_2 in the blood remain balanced

Exercise breathing

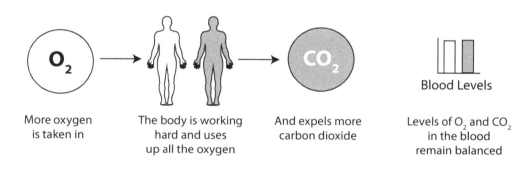

More oxygen is taken in | The body is working hard and uses up all the oxygen | And expels more carbon dioxide | Levels of O_2 and CO_2 in the blood remain balanced

Panic breathing

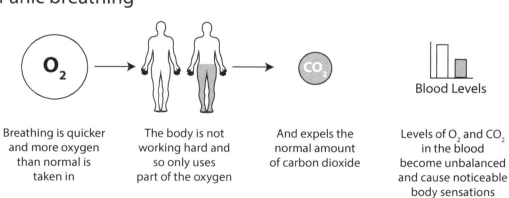

Breathing is quicker and more oxygen than normal is taken in | The body is not working hard and so only uses part of the oxygen | And expels the normal amount of carbon dioxide | Levels of O_2 and CO_2 in the blood become unbalanced and cause noticeable body sensations

Figure: Types of breathing.

When our breathing returns to its normal rate the levels of oxygen and carbon dioxide in the blood also return to normal, and the bodily symptoms resolve. By deliberately relaxing your breathing you can interrupt panic and kick-start the process of feeling better.

Relaxed breathing

Relaxed breathing signals to the body that there is no danger and that it is safe to relax. Breathing in this way helps us to reverse the fight-flight-freeze response. Anxious breathing is quick, shallow, forceful, and high up in the chest –it is all about forcing as much oxygen into your body as quickly as possible. By contrast, relaxed breathing is slower and deeper than normal breathing. Relaxed breathing happens lower in the body – typically the belly will move rather than the chest.

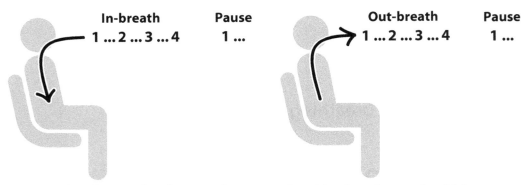

Figure: To breathe in a relaxed way try slowing your breathing down by counting. Make sure that your breaths are steady and continuous, not jerky.

Instructions for relaxed breathing

Follw the instructions below to practice relaxed breathing. If you find it difficult, or don't notice much change to begin with – keep trying. Relaxed breathing is a skill which develops with practice, and it may take time to notice the full effects.

1. Begin by sitting or lying comfortably. Try to make sure that you won't be disturbed for a few minutes.

2. Close your eyes if you are comfortable doing so.

3. If it feels comfortable, try to breathe through your nose rather than your mouth.

4. Try to find a natural breathing rhythm and just spend a few moments noticing yourself breathing without trying to control it.

5. Now gradually and deliberately start to slow down your breathing.

6. Make sure that your breaths are smooth, steady, and continuous - not jerky.

7. Aim to breathe in for a count of 4, pause briefly, and breathe out for a count of 4.

8. Pay particular attention to your out-breath - make sure that it is smooth, steady, and continuous.

Am I doing it right? What should I be paying attention to?

Relaxed breathing should be low down in the abdomen (belly), and not high in the chest. You can check this by putting one hand on your stomach and one on your chest. Try to keep the top hand still as you breathe - your breathing should move the bottom hand more than the top hand.

Focus your attention on your breath - some people find it helpful to count in their head to begin with (*"In … two … three … four … pause … out … two … three … four … pause …"*).

How long and how often?

Try breathing in a relaxed way for at least a few minutes at a time - it might take a few minutes for your to notice an effect. If you are comfortable, aim for 5-10 minutes. Set a timer so that you are not tempted to stop too soon.

Try to practice regularly, perhaps three times a day. If you practice relaxation regularly you will find that your general stress levels decrease and you will be less prone to experiencing panic attacks.

Variations and troubleshooting

Find a slow breathing rhythm that is comfortable for you. Counting to 4 isn't an absolute rule. Try 3 or 5. The important thing is that the breathing is slow and steady.

When they try to slow their breathing down some people find that their breathing can become a bit jerky. If this is the case then stop trying to control your breathing and just settle into a breathing rhythm that feels natural to you. Once you are breathing in a steady rhythm you can start to slow this down.

Some people find the sensation of relaxing to be unusual or uncomfortable at first, but this normally passes with practice. If you find it uncomfortable at first, or if you do not notice anything to begin with, do persist and keep practising.

Recording your practice and progress

Like learning any skill, relaxed breathing require practice. To begin with, it is best to practice regularly at times when you are not panicking. This way you will learn the skill, and will be able to use it more easily if you do begin to panic.

Breathing Record Form

Date	Anxiety before (0-100)	Length of time I practiced breathing	Anxiety after (0-100)
1st January	80	10 minutes	60
2nd January	30	5 minutes	10
3rd January	60	5 minutes	60
4th January	50	7 minutes	10
5th January	70	20 minutes	20
6th January	40	10 minutes	10
7th January	40	10 minutes	0

Figure: Ted's relaxed breathing record form.

Use the relaxed breathing record form on the next page to record your practice. Notice how anxious or stressed you feel before your practice and record it, then record how you feel after a relaxed breathing practice. Try to practice three times a day for at least a week. Many people find that practising relaxation in this way makes them less likely to experience panic. Once you have had some practice using this technique you may also find it a helpful way of keeping calm in anxiety-provoking situations.

Relaxed Breathing Record Form

Date & Time	Anxiety before (0-100%)	Length of time I practiced breathing	Anxiety after (0-100%)

Figure: Relaxed breathing record form. You will find blank copies at the back of this book, and you can download more forms from Psychology Tools (http://psychologytools.com)

Step 6: Working with anxious thoughts and predictions

Everyone has an emotional side and a rational side to their mind. Our emotional side says things like *"I'll go mad if this carries on"* and *"I'll die if I can't escape"*. The emotional side tends to make quick instinctive judgements about situations, but it isn't always correct. The rational side says things like *"It's very unlikely you'll go mad - it's never happened before"* and *"Just relax, you're not in any danger"*. Psychologists have found that it costs us more effort to use the rational side of our minds and so people tend to use it less often, especially if they are in stressful situations. Overcoming panic means nurturing and paying more attention to the rational side of our minds.

Panic gets worse when our emotional side becomes too loud or too convincing. When the emotional side of our brain causes a panic it makes 3 big mistakes:

- Mistake 1: it overestimates the chances of a catastrophe happening

- Mistake 2: it overestimates how awful it would be if that catastrophe happened

- Mistake 3: it underestimates our ability to cope if that catastrophe really did happen

Overcoming panic means correcting these mistakes. This is called *decatastrophizing*. Decatastrophizing is a skill that we can all learn to use. First you should practice using the decatastrophizing worksheet to think about your past experiences of panic. Once you have mastered the steps you should begin to use them as prompts to guide your thinking during a panic.

Decatastrophizing

To overcome catastrophic thinking it is helpful to use a decatastophizing worksheet. This teaches you to look at a problem using your rational side. To begin, let's think about Ted's experience.

Ted had a panic attack while he was in a shopping centre. He was worried that he was going to pass out - his anxious mind predicted that he would faint if he kept feeling so hot. Prompted by the questions on the decatastrophizing worksheet Ted asked himself how likely it would be that he really would faint. He had fainted once in the past so it wasn't entirely impossible, but he had been ill at the time and he wasn't ill currently. He told himself that his worry wasn't very realistic. He thought about how awful it would be if he did faint. He was reassured to think that even if it did happen he was in a public place and would probably be taken care of. He remembered that the last time he hadn't passed out for long, and had felt better once he had drunk some water. He thought about all the positive things he could do to cope if he really did feel faint, like sitting down, drinking water, or eating a snack, and he started to feel a bit better. Finally, Ted thought about what kind of reassuring things he would say to a friend if they were worried about something similar. He felt better when he said these things to himself, especially when he spoke to himself softly and petiently like is mother had wne he got upset as a child. He noticed that his anxiety reduced the more he reassured himself.

Ted's decatastrophizing worksheet is on the next page. Once you have read through Ted's example follow the instructions on the next page to use decatastrophizing for yourself.

Decatastrophizing Worksheet

What is the catastrophe that I am worried about?
Clearly state: What am I worried will happen? What am I predicting will happen?
Change any *"what if ... ?"* statements into clear predictions about what you fear will happen

I feel hot - If I stay here I'm going to pass out

Rate how awful you believe this catastrophe will be (0-100%)

90%

How *likely* is this event to happen?
Has anything this bad ever happened to you before?
How often does this kind of thing happen to you?
Realistically, is this likely to happen now?

I have fainted once - but I had food poisoning at the time - I don't have that now

Realistically, it's not likely to happen now

How *awful* would it be if this did happen?
What is the worst case scenario?
What is the best case scenario?
What would a friend say to me about my worry?

The worst that could happen is that I could fall and hit my head

Even if I did faint I'm not likely to die from it. The worst might be that I have

to go to hospital for a check-up

Just supposing the worst did happen, what would I do to *cope*?
Has anything similar happened before? How did I cope then?
Who or what could I call on to help me get through it?
What resources, skills, or abilities would be helpful to me if it did happen?

I tend to have some warning so could sit down if it did happen. I have my

mobile phone and could call my wife for help.

What positive & reassuring thing do you want to say to yourself about the 'catastrophe' now?
What would I like to hear to reassure me?
What tone of voice would I want to hear that reassurance in?

Although I feel hot I'm unlikely to faint. It's more
likely to be symptoms of my fight-or-flight reaction
going off at the wrong time - it's not dangerous

Rate how awful you believe this catastrophe will be now (0-100%)

30%

Figure: Ted's decatastrophising worksheet

Now let's try the same procedure on your last panic attack. Think back to the last time you had a panic attack and try to fill in the blank decatastrophizing worksheet on the next page. To start with, identify what you were worried was going to happen. You may already have a good idea about the kinds of things you panic about from the panic diaries you completed earlier. Questions to ask yourself include:

- What was the catastrophe that I was worried about?

- What was I worried would happen?

- What was I trying to prevent happen?

- How awful do you think the catastrophe will be (0-100%)?

Next we have to activate the logical part of our mind and think realistically about that catastrophe. The next box prompts you to think about how likely the catastrophe really is, how bad it might be, and what you would be able to do to cope if the worst did happen. Try to answer these questions. A helpful extra question to ask yourself here is:

- What would a good friend say to me about this if I told them my worry?

The last box is the important. When we are anxious what helps us most is to be reassured. This is why good friends offer reassurance instead of saying *"pull yourself together"* and it is what a caring parent will say to their upset child. Using what you know now about how realistic the catastrophe is, and thinking about the ways you would cope if something did happen, write down what you could say that would make you feel reassured. If you find this difficult try asking yourself:

- What would I say to a friend who was struggling with a similar issue?

Decatastrophizing Worksheet

What is the catastrophe that I am worried about?

Clearly state: What am I worried will happen? What am I predicting will happen?
Change any *"what if ... ?"* statements into clear predictions about what you fear will happen

Rate how awful you believe this catastrophe will be (0-100%)

How *likely* is this event to happen?

Has anything this bad ever happened to you before?
How often does this kind of thing happen to you?
Realistically, is this likely to happen now?

How *awful* would it be if this did happen?

What is the worst case scenario?
What is the best case scenario?
What would a friend say to me about my worry?

Just supposing the worst did happen, what would I do to *cope*?

Has anything similar happened before? How did I cope then?
Who or what could I call on to help me get through it?
What resources, skills, or abilities would be helpful to me if it did happen?

What positive & reassuring thing do you want to say to yourself about the 'catastrophe' now?

What would I like to hear to reassure me?
What tone of voice would I want to hear that reassurance in?

Rate how awful you believe this catastrophe will be now (0-100%)

Figure: Decatastrophizing worksheet. You will find blank copies at the back of this book, and you can download more forms from Psychology Tools (http://psychologytools.com)

You can use the worksheet to prompt you to ask these helpful questions during a panic attack. Once you have practised the process a few times using the worksheet you might find it helpful to carry this decatasrophizing flashcard with you. It will guide you through some helpful decatastrophizing questions should you have a panic. With practice it will become second nature to ask yourself these questions.

De-Catastrophizing

What am I **worried** is going to happen?

How **likely** is it to happen?
How many times has this thing NOT happened?

Realistically (without exaggerating) what is the worst that is likely to happen?

What would I do to **cope** if the worst did happen?

What **reassuring** thing can I say to myself now?

Figure: Decatastrophizing flashcard. Carry this with you and talk yourself through these steps whenever you feel a panic coming on. You will find blank copies at the back of this book, and you can download more forms from Psychology Tools (http://psychologytools.com)

Step 7: Coping with body sensations

When we have a panic attack our body's fight-flight-freeze system gets our body ready to cope with danger. People with panic often become scared of these body sensations, even though they are perfectly normal. Thought of like this, panic disorder is really the fear of particular body sensations. Fears of body sensations can be kept going because of:

- Catastrophic misinterpretation - Having negative thoughts about what the body sensations are, and what they mean, increases the level of panic

- Avoidance - Trying to avoid having the body sensations means that you have fewer opportunities to learn about how dangerous they truly are

How do we overcome fears? Psychologists use a variety of techniques, but the most effective ones all involve some exposure to the thing that we are afraid of: we have to face our fears. When we face a fear 'out there' in the world it is called *exposure*. But how do we face a body sensation? The best way is to do exercises which are designed to bring on particular body sensations. By bringing the body sensations on in a controlled fashion you have a chance to learn more about them. Psychologists call this practice *interoceptive exposure*.

Instructions for interoceptive exposure

The interoceptive exposure tasks in this section are intended to produce a variety of feelings in your body. Remember that they are not dangerous - some of them are similar to playground games that children play - but they can induce moderate feelings of discomfort. Try all of the exercises to begin with, one at a time, to find out which sensations your panic responds to. Read the instructions for each exercise, including how long you're supposed to carry out each task for. After each exercise write down what body symptoms and thoughts you noticed yourself having, and record how anxious you got. A record of Ted's interoceptive exposure practice is on the next page.

Interoceptive Exposure Worksheet

⚠️ **If you have any health concerns, or physical health problems, then you should speak to your doctor about the suitability of these exercises for you before you attempt them. They are designed to be uncomfortable, but should not be painful.**

Activity		Symptoms & Thoughts What did you notice in your body? What went through your mind?	Anxiety (0-100%)
Breathing Overbreathe *Breathe forcefully, fast and deep*	🕐 1 min	*Felt lightheaded* *Thought I would pass out*	*90%*
Breathe through a straw *Hold your nose and breathe through a drinking straw*	🕐 2 min		
Hold your breath	🕐 30 sec		
Physical exercise Run quickly on the spot *Lift your knees high*	🕐 2 min	*Felt sweaty and hot* *Not too worried*	*50%*
Step up and down on a stair *Hold on to the handrail for balance*	🕐 2 min		
Tense all body muscles	🕐 1 min		
Spinning & shaking Spin while sitting in an office chair *As fast as you can*	🕐 1 min	*Felt very dizzy for about a minute* *Worried it might not stop*	*70%*
Spin around while standing up *Make sure to leave yourself enough space & have a place to sit after*	🕐 1 min		
Shake your head from side to side *Then look straight ahead. Keep your eyes open.*	🕐 30 sec		
Head-rush Put your head between your legs then *sit up quickly*	🕐 1 min	*Felt woozy* *Reminded of when I did collapse*	*90%*
Lie down & relax for at least one minute then *sit up quickly*	🕐 1 min		
Unreality Stare at yourself in a mirror *Concentrate hard without blinking*	🕐 2 min	*Felt normal* *No worry at all*	*10%*
Stare at a blank wall *Concentrate hard without blinking*	🕐 2 min		
Stare at a fluorescent light and then try to read something	🕐 1 min		

Figure: Ted's interoceptive exposure worksheet.

Rules for interoceptive exposure

- Try to complete each task for the allotted time

- Stopping early counts as avoiding - try not to let your feelings get the better of you

- Focus on the sensations you experience during the interoceptive exposure and let yourself experience them fully- try not to distract yourself

Troubleshooting

Problem	Suggested solution
I want to do these exercises but I can't get started	It takes courage to attempt these exercises. Could you find a way to break it down and make it easier? Perhaps to begin with you could do the exercises with a trusted friend?
I don't like the feeling of panic that it brings on	You have a difficult choice to make. In the short term these exercises can be uncomfortable. Remind yourself that they are not dangerous, and think about the long-term advantages in overcoming your panic.

Precautions for interoceptive exposure

These exercises are not dangerous, although they can produce moderate feelings of discomfort. You should be in generally good health to attempt these exercises. If you have any of the following medical conditions, or any concerns about your health, then you should check with your doctor before trying them:

- Epilepsy or seizures

- Cardiac (heart) problems

- Asthma or lung problems

- Pregnant

- Neck problems, back problems, or other physical difficulties

Interoceptive Exposure

⚠ If you have any health concerns, or physical health problems, then you should speak to your doctor about the suitability of these exercises for you before you attempt them. They are designed to be uncomfortable, but should not be painful.

Activity		Symptoms & Thoughts What did you notice in your body? What went through your mind?	Anxiety (0-100)
Breathing Overbreathe *Breathe forcefully, fast and deep*	🕐 1 min		
Breathe through a straw *Hold your nose and breathe through a drinking straw*	🕐 2 min		
Hold your breath	🕐 30 sec		
Physical exercise Run quickly on the spot *Lift your knees high*	🕐 2 min		
Step up and down on a stair *Hold on to a handrail for balance*	🕐 2 min		
Tense all body muscles	🕐 1 min		
Spinning & shaking Spin while sitting in an office chair *As fast as you can*	🕐 1 min		
Spin around while standing up *Make sure to leave yourself enough space & have a place to sit after*	🕐 1 min		
Shake your head from side to side *Then look straight ahead. Keep your eyes open.*	🕐 30 sec		
Head-rush Put your head between your legs then *sit up quickly*	🕐 1 min		
Lie down & relax for at least one minute then *sit up quickly*	🕐 1 min		
Unreality Stare at yourself in a mirror *Concentrate hard without blinking*	🕐 2 min		
Stare at a blank wall *Concentrate hard without blinking*	🕐 2 min		
Stare at a fluorescent light and then *try to read something*	🕐 1 min		

Figure: Interoceptive exposure worksheet. You will find blank copies at the back of this book, and you can download more forms from Psychology Tools (http://psychologytools.com)

Rethinking your body sensations

Once you have tried all of the interoceptive exposure exercises a few times it is helpful to think again about body sensations you have associated with your panic. Spend some time thinking about body sensations you have experienced in previous panic attacks and what thoughts those sensations led to at the time. Think about what those sensations mean to you now. Fill in the table below – for each body sensation think about what would be the most likely reason for you experiencing that sensation in your day-to-day life.

Body sensation	Most likely reasons for me experiencing this sensation
Sweating	
Heart racing	
Out of breath	
Lightheaded	
Trembling	
Nausea or stomach distess	
Chills or hot flushes	
Numbness or tingling	
Feeling of unreality	
Chest pain or discomfort	

Step 8: Approach instead of avoiding

In part 2 we found out that avoidance is a key part of what keeps panic going. Of course it is a natural human reaction to want to avoid threatening situations (and uncomfortable body sensations). Avoiding often brings us a strong feeling of relief in the short term. Relief feels good and makes us more likely to use avoidance again in the future. Unfortunately avoidance also comes with costs. When we start to avoid things it can shrink the number of places that it feels 'safe' to go. It can cut us off from rewarding experiences, and avoidance can quickly make us feel less competent.

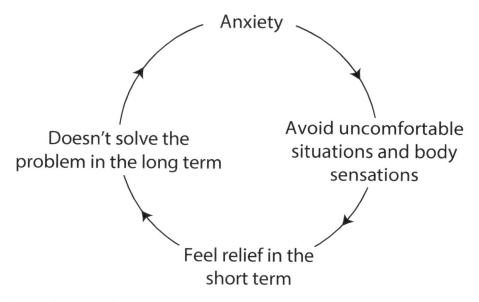

Figure: Anxiety and panic is maintained by avoidance of situations and body sensations

A key step in overcoming panic is to reverse the cycle of avoidance and to start to re-claim your old life. This might mean facing your fears and revisiting places where you have panicked, or re-trying activities that you have stopped because of the panic.

One of the best ways to tackle avoidance is *gradually*. It is helpful to begin by constructing a ladder of places or situations that you avoid. At the top of the ladder put the places or situations which make you most afraid. At the bottom of the ladder put places or situations you avoid, but which don't bother you as much. In the middle of the ladder put places or situations that are 'in-between'. Give each item a rating from 0-100% according to how anxious it would make you if you had to be in that situation.

To overcome your anxiety you will need to face your fears and approach these anxiety-provoking situations. Start with the places or situations at the bottom of your ladder and gradually work upwards. Don't move up the list too quickly. Wait until you feel more comfortable doing each item before moving on to the next.

Vanessa's avoidance ladder is on the next page. Once you have read Vanessa's example try to complete your own avoidance ladder on the following page.

Avoidance Hierarchy

Construct a ladder of places, situations, or events that you avoid. At the top of the ladder put those which which make you most anxious. At the bottom of the ladder put those you avoid, but which don't bother you as much. In the middle of the ladder put ones that are 'in-between'. Give each item a rating from 0-100% according to how anxious you would feel if you had to be in that situation. Overcome your anxiety by approaching these situations, starting from the bottom of the ladder.

Situation	Anxiety (0-100%)
Driving with the children in the car	100%
Driving on my own	90%
Exercising - going for a run	85%
Going to the shopping centre on my own	80%
Going to the shopping centre with my husband	75%
Looking after the children on my own	75%
Climbing stairs quickly	50%

Figure: Vanessa's avoidance hierarchy.

Avoidance Hierarchy

Construct a ladder of places, situations, or events that you avoid. At the top of the ladder put those which which make you most anxious. At the bottom of the ladder put those you avoid, but which don't bother you as much. In the middle of the ladder put ones that are 'in-between'. Give each item a rating from 0-100% according to how anxious you would feel if you had to be in that situation. Overcome your anxiety by approaching these situations, starting from the bottom of the ladder.

	Situation	Anxiety (0-100%)
	_____	_____
	_____	_____
	_____	_____
	_____	_____
	_____	_____
	_____	_____
	_____	_____
	_____	_____
	_____	_____
	_____	_____
	_____	_____
	_____	_____
	_____	_____

Figure: Avoidance hierarchy worksheet. You will find blank copies at the back of this book, and you can download more forms from Psychology Tools (http://psychologytools.com)

Step 9: Testing anxious and panicky predictions

Thoughts we have when we panic tend to be predictions or opinions, not facts. Panicky thoughts like these bring strong emotions along with them which can mistake us into thinking that they are true. Problems occur when we act as though these thoughts are facts.

For example, when Ted was in a crowded room he would have the panic thought *"If I stay in here I'm going to pass out"*. This thought was a prediction about Ted's future, but not an accurate one. Ted was healthy and had only fainted once before when he was really ill with flu. Ted was not aware how difficult it is for most people to faint if they are anxious. His panicky feelings were due to his fight-flight-freeze response – but they were not dangerous.

Ted's therapist suggested that it might be helpful for him to test how accurate some of his panicky predictions were. If they turned out to be accurate then he would have to find a way to live with them, but if they turned out to be inaccurate then Ted might not have to pay these thoughts so much attention.

One helpful way of testing predictions and beliefs is to carry out an experiment. When scientists carry out experiments they first make a prediction, then carry out an experiment which lets them test whether that prediction is true or false. When psychologists and CBT therapists carry out these experiments they call them *behavioral experiments*. Typical predictions in panic that can be tested include:

- *"Unless I get out of here then I will faint"*

- *"If I don't get out of this crowd I'll go crazy and start shouting"*

- *"If I go to that shop I will get so dizzy I will fall over"*

- *"If I don't stop feeling so scared I'll have a heart attack"*

- *"People will notice that I'm acting strangely and will think I'm weird"*

Ted's behavioral experiment

Ted was worried that he would faint if he had to go back to the hospital - the scene of his first panic attack. His prediction was that he would get, hot, short of breath, and would faint. For his behavioral experiment he made a plan that he would return to the hospital with a friend and would retrace his steps. He felt very anxious when he first arrived, had some strong memories of the previous time, and felt the start of his panic symptoms. However, the catastrophe he was worried about did not happen. Ted learned that he could manage his feeling of anxiety by reassuring himself, breathing calmly, and reminding himself of what he had learned. The longer he stayed, the less anxious he became. He started to feel more confident.

Ted's behavioral experiment form is on the next page. Once you have read through Ted's example follow the instructions on the next page to plan your own behavioral experiment.

Behavioral Experiment Worksheet

Prediction
What is your prediction?
What do you expect will happen?
How would you know if it came true?

If I go back to the hospital I will get really hot, short of breath, and will faint

Rate how strongly you believe this will happen (0-100%)

90%

Experiment
What experiment could test this prediction? (where & when)
What safety behaviors will need to be dropped?
How would you know your prediction had come true?

I will have to stop avoiding it and go to the hospital
I would know my prediction had come true if I faint, or if I wake up in hospital

Outcome
What happened?
Was your prediction accurate?

I went to the hospital with a friend
I was nervous and did feel hot to begin with. I wanted to leave but my friend encouraged me to stay. I felt less nervous after a time
My prediction was only partly accurate - I felt nervous and hot but I didn't faint

Learning
What did you learn?
How likely is it that your predictions will happen in the future?

I learnt that I can manage my feelings of anxiety if I hold my nerve and give them time to pass.

Rate how strongly you agree with your original prediction now (0-100%)

40%

Figure: Ted' behavioral experiment form.

Steps in carrying out a behavioral experiment

We will use a behavioral experiment form to plan and carry out your own experiments. There are four parts to a behavioral experiment. Once you have worked through the first two sections of the form systematically ('Prediction' and 'Experiment') it will be time to carry out your experiment. Complete the last two sections afterwards ('Outcome' and 'Learning').

Step 1: Prediction

Clearly state what you are predicting. Try to be as specific as you can. Instead of saying something general like *"I think something bad will happen"* try to work out specifically what the emotional side of your mind is worried is going to happen. Good specific ideas might include *"If I carry on feeling like that I'll lose my mind and be permanently damaged"* or *"I'll sweat uncontrollably and people will notice"*.

Step 2: Experiment

Before you carry out any experiment you have to set the rules up in advance. The first thing to do is to decide how to test the prediction. Think about:

- How could you test whether this prediction is accurate or not?

- What would you need to do to test the prediction?

If you have trouble thinking of a way to test your anxious prediction a good tip is to ask yourself *"What is the opposite of what I would normally do?"*. For Ted this meant actually going to the hospital, rather than avoiding it. Once you have a rough plan try to refine your idea by asking yourself the following questions:

- What would happen if the prediction was true?

- What would happen if the prediction was false?

- What would you need to observe?

- How many times will you have to the expriment in order for it to be a fair test?

- Sometimes people carry out a behavioral experiment and afterwards say "*Well, the catastrophe didn't happen but only because I was doing ...*". What safety behaviors would you have to stop using in order to make it a fair test?

Step 3: Outcome

Make sure to record what happens as soon afterwards as possible. It is important to decide beforehand what result you're looking for, and how you would know if the prediction has come true. The best experiments are ones that you carry out a number of times in order to get a fair result.

Step 4: Learning

Once you have carried your your experiment a number of times, think carefully about what you have learned.

- Did the prediction come true exactly as you said it would?

- If not, what did happen?

- What does the result tell you about the anxious predictions that the emotional side of your mind makes?

Behavioral Experiment Worksheet

Prediction
What is your prediction?
What do you expect will happen?
How would you know if it came true?

Rate how strongly you believe this will happen (0-100%)

Experiment
What experiment could test this prediction? (where & when)
What safety behaviors will need to be dropped?
How would you know your prediction had come true?

Outcome
What happened?
Was your prediction accurate?

Learning
What did you learn?
How likely is it that your predictions will happen in the future?

Rate how strongly you agree with your original prediction now (0-100%)

Figure: Behavioral experiment worksheet. You will find blank copies at the back of this book, and you can download more forms from Psychology Tools (http://psychologytools.com)

Part 4

What next?

How do I stop panic from coming back?

Once you have faced some of your fears and have decreased how often you experience panic it is natural to want to stay well. Psychologists find it helpful to complete a 'therapy blueprint' which helps you to consolidate everything that you have learned. Take some time to answer the questions below:

What have I learned about my panic?
What do I know about it now that I didn't know before?

What kinds of anxious predictions does my mind make when I panic?

How often have those predictions really come true?

What helps to calm me down?

What are my unhelpful safety behaviors?

If I could speak to my earlier, more panicky, self what would I say?

Dealing with setbacks

Recovering from panic is not easy, and it is possible that you will have setbacks along the way. You might even find that facing your fears leads to more anxiety in the short term. The more you practice the exercises in this book the easier you will find them, but you might still have days where it feels like you are going backwards.

Recovery is rarely smooth. We always wish that patterns of recovery would look like the first graph, but actual recovery more often looks like the second.

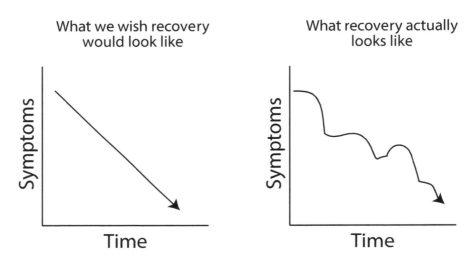

Figure: The path to recovery is rarely smooth

Even if you are having a bad day try not to become disheartened. Always remember that practising the exercises will lead you in the direction of recovery.

More information

Blank worksheets

The exercises in this book have relied upon a number of worksheets:

- Panic attack record form

- Panic attack mood diary

- Panic attack progress record

- Breathing record form

- Decatastrophizing record

- Decatastrophizing flashcard

- Interoceptive exposure record

- Avoidance hierarchy

- Behavioral experiment record

- Therapy blueprint for panic

There are blank worksheets that you can cut out and use at the back of the book. You can download and print more blank forms for free from the website Psychology Tools (http://psychologytools.com)

Further self-help

The website Psychology Tools (http://psychologytools.com) has a self-help section for panic disorder which includes clear up-to-date advice about how to deal with symptoms of anxiety and panic. If you have found any of the information or techniques in this book helpful then keep using them.

Professional help

Sometimes anxiety is stubborn, and it can be helpful to speak to someone about it. Good places to start include your family doctor or general practitioner, or a mental health professional such as a psychologist or psychiatrist. Cognitive behavioral therapy (CBT) is an evidence-based psychological therapy which is recommended for the treatment of panic. Research has shown that CBT is an effective treatment for panic when delivered by a qualified professional. UK government guidelines suggest that 7-14 hours of therapy is thought of as the optimal range for most people.

Medication

Two classes of medications have been shown to be helpful in the treatment of panic disorder:

- Selective Serotonin Re-uptake Inhibitors (SSRI's). These these are often just called 'antidepressants' but they are also effective for reducing anxi ety

- Tricyclic Antidepressants. These are an older class of antidepressant drug which also acts on anxiety

Certain medications have been associated with poorer long-term outcomes in panic disorder and are not recommended. These include benzodiazepines, sedating antihistamines, and antipsychotic medications.

Speak to your doctor for further information about medication.

Part 5

Appendix

Panic Attack Record

Date & Time	Fear rating (0-100%)

Situation Where were you? Who were you with?	Trigger What do you think caused your panic to start at that moment?
Ely/shopping Just got out car)	losing control seemed an awful long way to post letter a walkway (prediction)

Symptoms

- ☑ Heart pounding, racing, or palpitations
- ☐ Sweating
- ☐ Trembling or shaking
- ☑ Shortness of breath
- ☐ Feeling of choking
- ☐ Chest pain or discomfort
- ☐ Nausea or stomach distress
- ☐ Dizziness, lightheadedness, or feeling faint
- ☐ Chills or hot flushes
- ☐ Numbness or tingling
- ☐ Feelings of unreality
- ☐ Fear of losing control or going crazy
- ☑ Fear of dying

Thoughts (or images)
What was going through your mind?
What were you predicting would happen?

couldn't get to where I wanted to go

Coping strategy
What did you do to cope?
What action did you take to make yourself feel better?

Panic Attack Record

Date & Time	Fear rating (0-100%)

Situation	Trigger
Where were you? Who were you with?	What do you think caused your panic to start at that moment?

Symptoms

- ☐ Heart pounding, racing, or palpitations
- ☐ Sweating
- ☐ Trembling or shaking
- ☐ Shortness of breath
- ☐ Feeling of choking
- ☐ Chest pain or discomfort
- ☐ Nausea or stomach distress
- ☐ Dizziness, lightheadedness, or feeling faint
- ☐ Chills or hot flushes
- ☐ Numbness or tingling
- ☐ Feelings of unreality
- ☐ Fear of losing control or going crazy
- ☐ Fear of dying

Thoughts (or images)
What was going through your mind?
What were you predicting would happen?

Coping strategy
What did you do to cope?
What action did you take to make yourself feel better?

Panic Attack Record

Date & Time	Fear rating (0-100%)

Situation Where were you? Who were you with?	Trigger What do you think caused your panic to start at that moment?

Symptoms

- ☐ Heart pounding, racing, or palpitations
- ☐ Sweating
- ☐ Trembling or shaking
- ☐ Shortness of breath
- ☐ Feeling of choking
- ☐ Chest pain or discomfort
- ☐ Nausea or stomach distress
- ☐ Dizziness, lightheadedness, or feeling faint
- ☐ Chills or hot flushes
- ☐ Numbness or tingling
- ☐ Feelings of unreality
- ☐ Fear of losing control or going crazy
- ☐ Fear of dying

Thoughts (or images)
What was going through your mind?
What were you predicting would happen?

Coping strategy
What did you do to cope?
What action did you take to make yourself feel better?

Panic Attack Record

Date & Time	Fear rating (0-100%)

Situation Where were you? Who were you with?	Trigger What do you think caused your panic to start at that moment?

Symptoms

- ☐ Heart pounding, racing, or palpitations
- ☐ Sweating
- ☐ Trembling or shaking
- ☐ Shortness of breath
- ☐ Feeling of choking
- ☐ Chest pain or discomfort
- ☐ Nausea or stomach distress
- ☐ Dizziness, lightheadedness, or feeling faint
- ☐ Chills or hot flushes
- ☐ Numbness or tingling
- ☐ Feelings of unreality
- ☐ Fear of losing control or going crazy
- ☐ Fear of dying

Thoughts (or images)
What was going through your mind?
What were you predicting would happen?

Coping strategy
What did you do to cope?
What action did you take to make yourself feel better?

Panic Daily Mood Record

Record your mood every day so that you can monitor your progress. At the end of each week record your average scores on the panic attack progress record form.

Day / Date	Anxiety (0-100%) How anxious were you today?	Worry About Panic (0-100%) How much did you worry about having another panic attack?
Week __		
Week __		
Week __		
Week __		

Panic Daily Mood Record

Record your mood every day so that you can monitor your progress. At the end of each week record your average scores on the panic attack progress record form.

Day / Date	Anxiety (0-100%) How anxious were you today?	Worry About Panic (0-100%) How much did you worry about having another panic attack?
Week __		
Week __		
Week __		
Week __		

Panic Daily Mood Record

Record your mood every day so that you can monitor your progress. At the end of each week record your average scores on the panic attack progress record form.

Day / Date	Anxiety (0-100%) How anxious were you today?	Worry About Panic (0-100%) How much did you worry about having another panic attack?
Week __		
Week __		
Week __		
Week __		

Panic Daily Mood Record

Record your mood every day so that you can monitor your progress. At the end of each week record your average scores on the panic attack progress record form.

Day / Date	Anxiety (0-100%) How anxious were you today?	Worry About Panic (0-100%) How much did you worry about having another panic attack?
Week ___		
Week ___		
Week ___		
Week ___		

Panic Attack Progress Record

Regularly and accurately recording how you feel is very important in therapy.
You should make the habit of doing it every day in order to obtain the most benefit.

Recording your symptoms every day:
- ✓ Gives you more accurate information compared to just asking yourself *"how have I been feeling lately?"*
- ✓ Allows you to evaluate your progress over time

The forms on the following pages allow you to record details of any panic attacks you have, and your daily moods, for a month. You should complete a separate form for every panic attack.

Use the graphs below to record your progress at the end of each week.

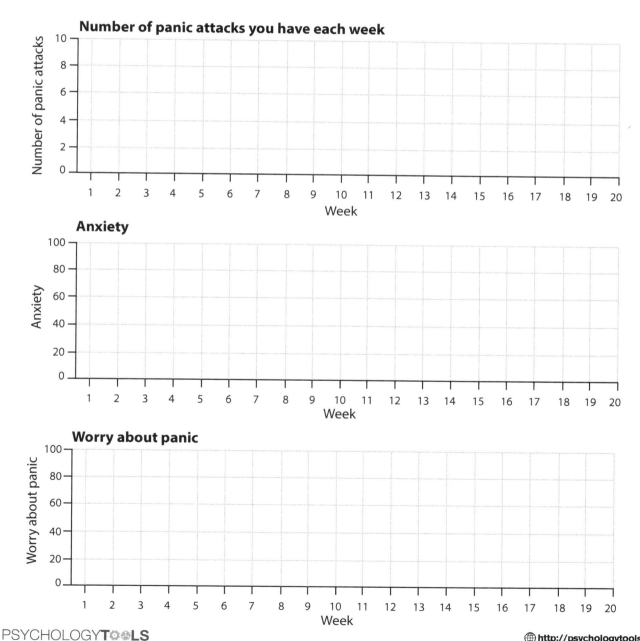

Panic Attack Progress Record

Regularly and accurately recording how you feel is very important in therapy.
You should make the habit of doing it every day in order to obtain the most benefit.

Recording your symptoms every day:
- ✓ Gives you more accurate information compared to just asking yourself *"how have I been feeling lately?"*
- ✓ Allows you to evaluate your progress over time

The forms on the following pages allow you to record details of any panic attacks you have, and your daily moods, for a month. You should complete a separate form for every panic attack.

Use the graphs below to record your progress at the end of each week.

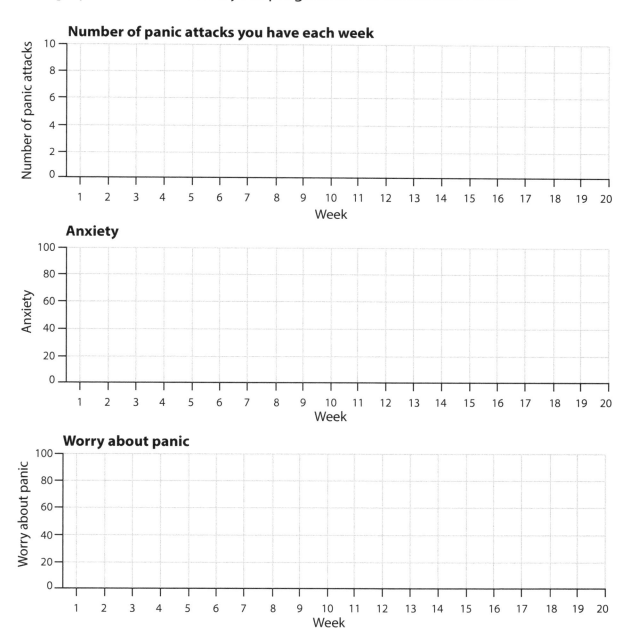

Relaxed Breathing Record Form

Date & Time	Anxiety before (0-100%)	Length of time I practiced breathing	Anxiety after (0-100%)

Relaxed Breathing Record Form

Date & Time	Anxiety before (0-100%)	Length of time I practiced breathing	Anxiety after (0-100%)

Relaxed Breathing Record Form

Date & Time	Anxiety before (0-100%)	Length of time I practiced breathing	Anxiety after (0-100%)

Relaxed Breathing Record Form

Date & Time	Anxiety before (0-100%)	Length of time I practiced breathing	Anxiety after (0-100%)

Relaxed Breathing Record Form

Date & Time	Anxiety before (0-100%)	Length of time I practiced breathing	Anxiety after (0-100%)

http://psychologytools.com

Decatastrophizing

What is the catastrophe that I am worried about?

Clearly state: What am I worried will happen? What am I predicting will happen?
Change any *"what if ... ?"* statements into clear predictions about what you fear will happen

Rate how awful you believe this catastrophe will be (0-100%)

How *likely* is this event to happen?

Has anything this bad ever happened to you before?
How often does this kind of thing happen to you?
Realistically, is this likely to happen now?

How *awful* would it be if this did happen?

What is the worst case scenario?
What is the best case scenario?
What would a friend say to me about my worry?

Just supposing the worst did happen, what would I do to *cope*?

Has anything similar happened before? How did I cope then?
Who or what could I call on to help me get through it?
What resources, skills, or abilities would be helpful to me if it did happen?

What positive & reassuring thing do you want to say to yourself about the 'catastrophe' now?

What would I like to hear to reassure me?
What tone of voice would I want to hear that reassurance in?

Rate how awful you believe this catastrophe will be now (0-100%)

Decatastrophizing

What is the catastrophe that I am worried about?
Clearly state: What am I worried will happen? What am I predicting will happen?
Change any *"what if ... ?"* statements into clear predictions about what you fear will happen

Rate how awful you believe this catastrophe will be (0-100%)

How *likely* is this event to happen?
Has anything this bad ever happened to you before?
How often does this kind of thing happen to you?
Realistically, is this likely to happen now?

How *awful* would it be if this did happen?
What is the worst case scenario?
What is the best case scenario?
What would a friend say to me about my worry?

Just supposing the worst did happen, what would I do to *cope*?
Has anything similar happened before? How did I cope then?
Who or what could I call on to help me get through it?
What resources, skills, or abilities would be helpful to me if it did happen?

What positive & reassuring thing do you want to say to yourself about the 'catastrophe' now?
What would I like to hear to reassure me?
What tone of voice would I want to hear that reassurance in?

Rate how awful you believe this catastrophe will be now (0-100%)

Decatastrophizing

What is the catastrophe that I am worried about?

Clearly state: What am I worried will happen? What am I predicting will happen?

Change any *"what if ... ?"* statements into clear predictions about what you fear will happen

Rate how awful you believe this catastrophe will be (0-100%)

How *likely* is this event to happen?

Has anything this bad ever happened to you before?

How often does this kind of thing happen to you?

Realistically, is this likely to happen now?

How *awful* would it be if this did happen?

What is the worst case scenario?

What is the best case scenario?

What would a friend say to me about my worry?

Just supposing the worst did happen, what would I do to *cope*?

Has anything similar happened before? How did I cope then?

Who or what could I call on to help me get through it?

What resources, skills, or abilities would be helpful to me if it did happen?

What positive & reassuring thing do you want to say to yourself about the 'catastrophe' now?

What would I like to hear to reassure me?

What tone of voice would I want to hear that reassurance in?

Rate how awful you believe this catastrophe will be now (0-100%)

Decatastrophizing

What is the catastrophe that I am worried about?

Clearly state: What am I worried will happen? What am I predicting will happen?
Change any *"what if ... ?"* statements into clear predictions about what you fear will happen

Rate how awful you believe this catastrophe will be (0-100%)

How *likely* is this event to happen?

Has anything this bad ever happened to you before?
How often does this kind of thing happen to you?
Realistically, is this likely to happen now?

How *awful* would it be if this did happen?

What is the worst case scenario?
What is the best case scenario?
What would a friend say to me about my worry?

Just supposing the worst did happen, what would I do to *cope*?

Has anything similar happened before? How did I cope then?
Who or what could I call on to help me get through it?
What resources, skills, or abilities would be helpful to me if it did happen?

What positive & reassuring thing do you want to say to yourself about the 'catastrophe' now?

What would I like to hear to reassure me?
What tone of voice would I want to hear that reassurance in?

Rate how awful you believe this catastrophe will be now (0-100%)

http://psychologytools.com

Decatastrophizing Flashcard

De-Catastrophizing

What am I **worried** is going to happen?

How **likely** is it to happen?
How many times has this thing NOT happened?

Realistically (without exaggerating) what is the worst that is likely to happen?

What would I do to **cope** if the worst did happen?

What **reassuring** thing can I say to myself now?

De-Catastrophizing

What am I **worried** is going to happen?

How **likely** is it to happen?
How many times has this thing NOT happened?

Realistically (without exaggerating) what is the worst that is likely to happen?

What would I do to **cope** if the worst did happen?

What **reassuring** thing can I say to myself now?

De-Catastrophizing

What am I **worried** is going to happen?

How **likely** is it to happen?
How many times has this thing NOT happened?

Realistically (without exaggerating) what is the worst that is likely to happen?

What would I do to **cope** if the worst did happen?

What **reassuring** thing can I say to myself now?

Interoceptive Exposure

⚠ **If you have any health concerns, or physical health problems, then you should speak to your doctor about the suitability of these exercises for you before you attempt them. They are designed to be uncomfortable, but should not be painful.**

Activity	Symptoms & Thoughts *What did you notice in your body?* *What went through your mind?*	Anxiety Rate 0-100%
Breathing Overbreathe *Breathe forcefully, fast and deep* 🕐 1 min		
Breathe through a straw *Hold your nose and breathe through a drinking straw* 🕐 2 min		
Hold your breath 🕐 30 sec		
Physical exercise Run quickly on the spot *Lift your knees high* 🕐 2 min		
Step up and down on a stair *Hold on to the handrail for balance* 🕐 2 min		
Tense all body muscles 🕐 1 min		
Spinning & shaking Spin while sitting in an office chair *As fast as you can* 🕐 1 min		
Spin around while standing up *Make sure to leave yourself enough space & have a place to sit after* 🕐 1 min		
Shake your head from side to side *Then look straight ahead. Keep your eyes open.* 🕐 30 sec		
Head-rush Put your head between your legs then *sit up quickly* 🕐 1 min		
Lie down & relax for at least one minute then *sit up quickly* 🕐 1 min		
Unreality Stare at yourself in a mirror *Concentrate hard without blinking* 🕐 2 min		
Stare at a blank wall *Concentrate hard without blinking* 🕐 2 min		
Stare at a fluorescent light and then *try to read something* 🕐 1 min		

Interoceptive Exposure

⚠️ **If you have any health concerns, or physical health problems, then you should speak to your doctor about the suitability of these exercises for you before you attempt them. They are designed to be uncomfortable, but should not be painful.**

Activity	Symptoms & Thoughts What did you notice in your body? What went through your mind?	Anxiety Rate 0-100%
Breathing Overbreathe *Breathe forcefully, fast and deep* — 🕐 1 min		
Breathe through a straw *Hold your nose and breathe through a drinking straw* — 🕐 2 min		
Hold your breath — 🕐 30 sec		
Physical exercise Run quickly on the spot *Lift your knees high* — 🕐 2 min		
Step up and down on a stair *Hold on to the handrail for balance* — 🕐 2 min		
Tense all body muscles — 🕐 1 min		
Spinning & shaking Spin while sitting in an office chair *As fast as you can* — 🕐 1 min		
Spin around while standing up *Make sure to leave yourself enough space & have a place to sit after* — 🕐 1 min		
Shake your head from side to side *Then look straight ahead. Keep your eyes open.* — 🕐 30 sec		
Head-rush Put your head between your legs then *sit up quickly* — 🕐 1 min		
Lie down & relax for at least one minute then *sit up quickly* — 🕐 1 min		
Unreality Stare at yourself in a mirror *Concentrate hard without blinking* — 🕐 2 min		
Stare at a blank wall *Concentrate hard without blinking* — 🕐 2 min		
Stare at a fluorescent light and then *try to read something* — 🕐 1 min		

Interoceptive Exposure

⚠️ **If you have any health concerns, or physical health problems, then you should speak to your doctor about the suitability of these exercises for you before you attempt them. They are designed to be uncomfortable, but should not be painful.**

Activity	Symptoms & Thoughts What did you notice in your body? What went through your mind?	Anxiety Rate 0-100%
Breathing Overbreathe *Breathe forcefully, fast and deep* 🕐 1 min		
Breathe through a straw *Hold your nose and breathe through a drinking straw* 🕐 2 min		
Hold your breath 🕐 30 sec		
Physical exercise Run quickly on the spot *Lift your knees high* 🕐 2 min		
Step up and down on a stair *Hold on to the handrail for balance* 🕐 2 min		
Tense all body muscles 🕐 1 min		
Spinning & shaking Spin while sitting in an office chair *As fast as you can* 🕐 1 min		
Spin around while standing up *Make sure to leave yourself enough space & have a place to sit after* 🕐 1 min		
Shake your head from side to side *Then look straight ahead. Keep your eyes open.* 🕐 30 sec		
Head-rush Put your head between your legs then *sit up quickly* 🕐 1 min		
Lie down & relax for at least one minute then *sit up quickly* 🕐 1 min		
Unreality Stare at yourself in a mirror *Concentrate hard without blinking* 🕐 2 min		
Stare at a blank wall *Concentrate hard without blinking* 🕐 2 min		
Stare at a fluorescent light and then *try to read something* 🕐 1 min		

Interoceptive Exposure

⚠️ If you have any health concerns, or physical health problems, then you should speak to your doctor about the suitability of these exercises for you before you attempt them. They are designed to be uncomfortable, but should not be painful.

Activity	Symptoms & Thoughts What did you notice in your body? What went through your mind?	Anxiety Rate 0-100%
Breathing Overbreathe *Breathe forcefully, fast and deep* 🕐 1 min		
Breathe through a straw *Hold your nose and breathe through a drinking straw* 🕐 2 min		
Hold your breath 🕐 30 sec		
Physical exercise Run quickly on the spot *Lift your knees high* 🕐 2 min		
Step up and down on a stair *Hold on to the handrail for balance* 🕐 2 min		
Tense all body muscles 🕐 1 min		
Spinning & shaking Spin while sitting in an office chair *As fast as you can* 🕐 1 min		
Spin around while standing up *Make sure to leave yourself enough space & have a place to sit after* 🕐 1 min		
Shake your head from side to side *Then look straight ahead. Keep your eyes open.* 🕐 30 sec		
Head-rush Put your head between your legs then *sit up quickly* 🕐 1 min		
Lie down & relax for at least one minute then *sit up quickly* 🕐 1 min		
Unreality Stare at yourself in a mirror *Concentrate hard without blinking* 🕐 2 min		
Stare at a blank wall *Concentrate hard without blinking* 🕐 2 min		
Stare at a fluorescent light and then *try to read something* 🕐 1 min		

Interoceptive Exposure

⚠️ If you have any health concerns, or physical health problems, then you should speak to your doctor about the suitability of these exercises for you before you attempt them. They are designed to be uncomfortable, but should not be painful.

Activity	Symptoms & Thoughts *What did you notice in your body?* *What went through your mind?*	Anxiety Rate 0-100%
Breathing		
Overbreathe *Breathe forcefully, fast and deep* 🕐 1 min		
Breathe through a straw *Hold your nose and breathe* *through a drinking straw* 🕐 2 min		
Hold your breath 🕐 30 sec		
Physical exercise		
Run quickly on the spot *Lift your knees high* 🕐 2 min		
Step up and down on a stair *Hold on to the handrail for balance* 🕐 2 min		
Tense all body muscles 🕐 1 min		
Spinning & shaking		
Spin while sitting in an office chair *As fast as you can* 🕐 1 min		
Spin around while standing up *Make sure to leave yourself enough* *space & have a place to sit after* 🕐 1 min		
Shake your head from side to side *Then look straight ahead. Keep your* *eyes open.* 🕐 30 sec		
Head-rush		
Put your head between your legs then *sit up quickly* 🕐 1 min		
Lie down & relax for at least one minute then *sit up quickly* 🕐 1 min		
Unreality		
Stare at yourself in a mirror *Concentrate hard without blinking* 🕐 2 min		
Stare at a blank wall *Concentrate hard without blinking* 🕐 2 min		
Stare at a fluorescent light and then *try to read something* 🕐 1 min		

Avoidance Hierarchy

Construct a ladder of places or situations that you avoid. At the top of the ladder put those which which make you most anxious. At the bottom of the ladder put places or situations you avoid, but which don't bother you as much. In the middle of the ladder put ones that are 'in-between'. Give each item a rating from 0-100% according to how anxious you would feel if you had to be in that situation. Overcome your anxiety by approaching these situations, starting from the bottom of the ladder.

Situation   Anxiety (0-100%)

_____   _____

_____   _____

_____   _____

_____   _____

_____   _____

_____   _____

_____   _____

_____   _____

_____   _____

_____   _____

_____   _____

_____   _____

_____   _____

Avoidance Hierarchy

Construct a ladder of places or situations that you avoid. At the top of the ladder put those which which make you most anxious. At the bottom of the ladder put places or situations you avoid, but which don't bother you as much. In the middle of the ladder put ones that are 'in-between'. Give each item a rating from 0-100% according to how anxious you would feel if you had to be in that situation. Overcome your anxiety by approaching these situations, starting from the bottom of the ladder.

Situation   Anxiety (0-100%)

_____   _____

_____   _____

_____   _____

_____   _____

_____   _____

_____   _____

_____   _____

_____   _____

_____   _____

_____   _____

_____   _____

_____   _____

_____   _____

Behavioral Experiment

Prediction
What is your prediction?
What do you expect will happen?
How would you know if it came true?

Rate how strongly you believe this will happen (0-100%)

Experiment
What experiment could test this prediction? (where & when)
What safety behaviors will need to be dropped?
How would you know your prediction had come true?

Outcome
What happened?
Was your prediction accurate?

Learning
What did you learn?
How likely is it that your predictions will happen in the future?

Rate how strongly you agree with your original prediction now (0-100%)

Behavioral Experiment

Prediction
What is your prediction?
What do you expect will happen?
How would you know if it came true?

Rate how strongly you believe this will happen (0-100%)

Experiment
What experiment could test this prediction? (where & when)
What safety behaviors will need to be dropped?
How would you know your prediction had come true?

Outcome
What happened?
Was your prediction accurate?

Learning
What did you learn?
How likely is it that your predictions will happen in the future?

Rate how strongly you agree with your original prediction now (0-100%)

Behavioral Experiment

Prediction
What is your prediction?
What do you expect will happen?
How would you know if it came true?

Rate how strongly you believe this will happen (0-100%)

Experiment
What experiment could test this prediction? (where & when)
What safety behaviors will need to be dropped?
How would you know your prediction had come true?

Outcome
What happened?
Was your prediction accurate?

Learning
What did you learn?
How likely is it that your predictions will happen in the future?

Rate how strongly you agree with your original prediction now (0-100%)

Behavioral Experiment

Prediction
What is your prediction?
What do you expect will happen?
How would you know if it came true?

Rate how strongly you believe this will happen (0-100%)

Experiment
What experiment could test this prediction? (where & when)
What safety behaviors will need to be dropped?
How would you know your prediction had come true?

Outcome
What happened?
Was your prediction accurate?

Learning
What did you learn?
How likely is it that your predictions will happen in the future?

Rate how strongly you agree with your original prediction now (0-100%)

Behavioral Experiment

Prediction

What is your prediction?
What do you expect will happen?
How would you know if it came true?

Rate how strongly you believe this will happen (0-100%)

Experiment

What experiment could test this prediction? (where & when)
What safety behaviors will need to be dropped?
How would you know your prediction had come true?

Outcome

What happened?
Was your prediction accurate?

Learning

What did you learn?
How likely is it that your predictions will happen in the future?

Rate how strongly you agree with your original prediction now (0-100%)

Therapy Blueprint For Panic

What have I learned about my panic?
What do I know about it now that I didn't know before?

What kinds of anxious predictions does my mind make when I panic?

How often have those predictions really come true?

What helps to calm me down?

What are my unhelpful safety behaviors?

If I could speak to my earlier, more panicky, self what would I say?

Therapy Blueprint For Panic

What have I learned about my panic?
What do I know about it now that I didn't know before?

What kinds of anxious predictions does my mind make when I panic?

How often have those predictions really come true?

What helps to calm me down?

What are my unhelpful safety behaviors?

If I could speak to my earlier, more panicky, self what would I say?

Lightning Source UK Ltd.
Milton Keynes UK
UKHW032052150419
341063UK00022B/599/P